THE WILD BOAR SPEAKS

THE WILD BOAR SPEAKS

THE COLLECTED POETRY OF
TASSOS DENEGRIS

TRANSLATED BY
PHILIP RAMP

All rights reserved. No part of this work covered by the copyright herein may be reproduced or used in any means – graphic, electronic, or mechanical, including copying, recording, taping, or information storage and retrieval systems – without written permission of the publisher.

Printed by imprintdigital
Upton Pyne, Exeter
www.digital.imprint.co.uk

Typesetting and cover design by narrator
www.narrator.me.uk
info@narrator.me.uk
033 022 300 39

Published by Shoestring Press
19 Devonshire Avenue, Beeston, Nottingham, NG9 1BS
(0115) 925 1827
www.shoestringpress.co.uk

First published 2017
© Copyright: Philip Ramp

The moral right of the author has been asserted.

ISBN 978-1-910323-44-1

Dedicated to my wife Ioanna Boufi Denegri

CONTENTS

About the Author 1
Instead of Prologue: the subject is never anything
other than you 3

DEATH IN KANINGOS SQUARE (1975) 5

Cold War 7
Sacred Way 8
White Horse 9
Elegy for Dead Youths 10
Epitaph 11
Death of an Old Woman Who Became a Nun 12
Procedure 13
The Example of Leonardos 14
Perversity 15
Four Poems for Eleni 16
Loukianou Street 17
The Spies 18
The Epileptic's Dilemma 19
Sex on the Brain 20
Ioanna 21
Unconditional 22
Close-up 23
Extreme Despair 24
The Assassination of Nikephoros Fokas 25
Verdict 27
High and Dry 28
The Generals 29
Faust and Indian Cannabis 30
My Participation in a Successful Rocket Launching 31
Equilibrium Is Maintained 32
Bossa Nova 33
Town Planning 34
Death in the Square 35
Lent 37
The Slivers of Day 38
The Coronation 39

Ballad for Jane Fonda	40
King's Palace Hotel	41
Greece, the Land of Miracles	42
Unnatural Procedure	43
6	44

THE BLOOD OF THE WOLF (1978) — 45

he Spirit of Bossa Nova	47
Momentary	48
Passion and Where It Leads Me	49
The Blood of the Wolf	50
Modus Vivendi	51
Signs and Wonders	52
Ostracism	53
Judgment Day	54
Spring Fever	55
Desperado Again	56
The Scandal	57
Traffic Accident	58
Anathema	59
Tyrants Should Be Afraid	60
Massacre in My Mind	61
Announcement	62
On Spring	63
Ode to a Photomodel	64
Kyrie Eleison	65
What I Have to Say about Emancipation	66
I Don't Know What to Say Anymore	67
Lilith	68
The Sun Sets as We Approach Patras	69
The Sweetness of Nihilism	70
Leveling	71
The Confusion Is General	72
Νύν Υπὲρ Πάντων Αγών	73
Priscilla	74

Sulfur and Apotheosis (1982) — 77

- The First Murder of the Cat — 79
- Sunset — 80
- Northern Suburbs — 81
- The Intruder — 82
- The River — 83
- The Great Paranoiac — 84
- I Love Peace but While I Am Speaking They Are Preparing for War — 85
- The Little Condottiero — 87
- Portrait of a Kindergarten Teacher — 88
- The Portent — 89
- Outside My Window — 91
- The Title Is Difficult — 92
- Mushroom of Night — 93
- My Dead Leader — 94
- Lucky Luciano — 95
- Interpretation of the Poem — 97
- Polyphonic — 98
- Sovereign Sky — 99
- The Foliage of Fear — 100
- Self-defense — 101
- The Forgotten Boat — 102
- Black Thorn — 104
- Pimp in a People's Court — 105
- Music Carried Me off — 107
- The Second Murder of the Cat — 108
- Her Eyes — 110
- Sunset in the Midwestern States — 111
- Impressions from a Reading of Poems in Japanese — 112
- On the Poem Again — 113
- Patriotism — 114
- Not to Mince Words — 115
- In the Sky — 116
- National Depression — 117
- Torture of a Citizen without Any Details — 118
- Confidences — 119
- Images from an Excursion — 120
- Cosmogony — 121

Instantaneously (1985) — 123

- October — 125
- Los Angeles — 127
- Postwar — 128
- Instantaneous — 130
- New Orleans — 131
- The Bright Idea — 132
- Invitation for Polo — 133
- Descending — 134
- Ritual — 135
- Saint John Rendis — 136
- September Moon — 137
- The Ugliness of a Day — 138
- The Ghoul — 139
- Summer Summary — 141
- The Wind Brings — 142
- The Same Otherwise — 143
- Countdown — 144
- Inmost — 145
- The Evolution of the Landscape — 146
- The Showdown — 147
- Untitled — 148
- A Day — 149
- Horrific Confirmation — 150
- The Other Version — 151
- Eloquent Puzzlement — 152
- Chrysostomos Smyrnis Street — 153
- The Beginning of Autumn — 154
- The Magical Procedure — 155
- The Barons of the Hospitals — 156
- Stable Point — 157
- Child's Poem — 158
- Disagreeable Poem — 159

The State of Things (1989) — 161

- The State of Things — 163
- Blurred Photograph — 164
- View from the Window — 165

Lightning Bolts	166
Ugliness of Civilization	167
Uncommon Snow	168
Bluntly	169
Zen	170
Eastern View	171
Ayia Marina, Attica	172
Essence of the Landscape	173
After a Sudden Rain	174
Spark	175
Dead End	176
Confession	177
Two Birch-trees Converse	178
31 December 1985	179
Aegina	180
Dematerialization	181
The Picture Blooms	182
Bitter Confirmation	183
Dublin	184

THE SPIRIT OF DEFENSE (1999) — 185

Two Sketches on Madness	187
I Am Something Inconceivable	188
I Was Struggling to Expel	189
Epitaph for the Hated Murderer Duft	191
The Straw in the Darkness	193
In Praise of the Moon	194
Perama	195
The Trauma Hospital	196
The Heat Wave of 1987	198
Games Time Plays	200
The Spirit of Defense	201
Nostalgia for the Future	202
Childhood Years	203
In the Park at the Old People's Home	204
High Fever	206
The December Incidents	207
Loukia	208

Solitude Sharpens the Senses	211
What a Pity	212
The Altar of the Homeland	213
Delicate Balances	214
Uninhibited Poem	215

THE WILD BOAR SPEAKS (2008) — 217

An Implacable Image	219
Strange Ideas	220
Elegy for the Fall of Constantinople	221
The Castle of Kythera	222
The Nightmares	224
In Memory of One Who Committed Suicide	226
Reggae	228
The Millenium Nears Its End	229
The Poem Knows Nothing of Obstacles	230
Relatives of the Victims Ascend	231
1998	232
Question	233
Commentary on the First Part of *The Deer Hunter*	234
Park in Stockholm	236
Days of November 2003	237
Outrageous Poem	238
Florence	239
Medellin	241
In Conclusion	242
The Wild Boar Speaks	243

AFTERWORD — 245

The Poetry of Tassos Denegris and Its "Generational" Axes	247
Note on the Translator	256
Note on Victor Ivanovici	256

ABOUT THE AUTHOR

Tassos Denegris was born in Athens in 1934. He graduated from Athens American College in 1953 and later studied cinema in Rome but in 1957 was forced, due to financial difficulties, to abandon his studies there. He went on to serve the Greek Army and, after his discharge, worked in the Greek film industry for two years. In 1962 he was appointed to the Prime Minister's Office, working in the Foreign Press Department. He resigned from his post in 1975.

Denegris made his first appearance in letters in 1952 with the poem "Conquest", published in "Strofi" ("Turn") magazine and went on to become a member of the editorial staff of the avant-garde magazine "Pali" ("Again"). He published seven collections of poetry ("Death in Kaningos Square", "The Blood of the Wolf", "Sulphur and Apotheosis", "Instantaneously", "The State of Things", "The Spirit of Defence" and "The Wild Boar Speaks"). In 1975 he became a Fellow at the International Writing Program, University of Iowa, and a member of the Greek Authors Society.

In 1983, he was guest poet at the Cambridge Poetry Festival in England and, in the following years, he red in Former Yugoslavia, India, Ireland, the United States, France, Germany, Spain, Colombia and Peru.

Denegris' contribution on translating major international authors into Greek, primarily from Spanish poetry and prose, is also memorable, including Borges, Cortazar, Vega, Lorca, O. Paz,I.B.Singer and several others. His own poems have been translated and published in a wide range of magazines and anthologies. In 1994 a selection of his poetry was published in Lisbon, entitled "A Outra Versao" (The Other Version"), while in 2000 another selection of his poems were published in England by Shoestring Press and in Malaga, Spain entitled "Flora Brutal". Tassos Denegris died in February 2009.

INSTEAD OF PROLOGUE: THE SUBJECT IS NEVER ANYTHING OTHER THAN YOU*

My relationship with poetry has its roots in my obsession with Time and History.

For me Time is neither a threat nor an ally but a terrible force that moves life. One of the most profound ambitions of poetry is capturing and arresting the moment, in order to reveal a glimpse of eternity, to do the one need to avoid the traps of rhetoric, by way of organizing language. Poetic time is stilled, it is at the antipodes of the flow of musical time: Brazilian music, the artful samba, the bossa-nova of Heitor Villa-Lobos, Antonio Carlos Zobim, Vinicius De Moraes.

I have always thought of history as a set of great contradictions, realistic and inexplicable at the same time. Inexplicable in terms of the generation of events, realistic in terms of its outcome. Just like painting. Spanish painting in particular: Velasquez, Goya, Picasso.

In my poems I do not choose characters in terms of a specific period since I regard history just like language, a ceaselessly developing process. I do not distinguish past from present. The elements that attract me are found in contradictory characters, the controversial nature of their acts and their tragic fate. Isolated from their historical context they acquire a new dimension. Furthermore, there is the unforeseen nature of Logos itself and the sense of freedom it entails, the same force that permits life to shape itself into forms. Wandering about in urban and natural landscapes, one's personal life, moral and aesthetic dilemmas, all acquire their meaning and their own special thematic weight; but perhaps greater than any other influence is the reading of other poets. You are the subject. You are identified with whatever is out there. Any influence limits itself to texture while, at the same time, the poet's final aspiration is to conquer a world of his own. This was the course of the like of: Kalvos, Solomos, Sikelianos,

---

* This is the last published writing of Tassos Denegris before his death, and is a marvelously clear and succinct statement on his beliefs: he clearly practiced what he preached.

Karyotakis, Engonopoulos, Rimbaud, Laforgue, Vallejo, Ashbery, Heaney. As a reader, however, I have mostly been swept away by prose, though it runs counter to poetry and its aim towards a 'close-knit' text. Prose depicts time more realistically and furthermore, through the element of plot, we are led to conclusions not left open to chance revelation: Papadiamantis, Kosmas Politis, Cervantes, Dostoyevsky, Faulkner, Rulfo, Cortazar, Sabato, Marquez, Cherniansky.

In the end comes translation, translating and being translated. I avail myself of this opportunity to mention the poets Fiama Ase Pais Brandao, Philip Ramp and Pedro Mateo who have honoured me with their translations into Portuguese, English and Spanish respectively. For me translation is like the siege of a foreign castle. It demands the drawing up of a military plan and it is twofold. The first is the language itself. The second is the purely creative process. The linguistic part requires a scholarly focus; the creative part requires inspiration and is intended to broaden the terms of the imagination. Same as travel: New Delhi, Belgrade, Stockholm, Dublin, Lisbon, Cordova, Rome, Chicago, New Orleans, Lima. To what degree my translations have influenced my poetry, what kind of interaction is there between translating and original work, is a mystery to me. This is particularly interesting in our times, where creative writing is consistently taught in universities worldwide. What I know is that there would be no poetry without 'passion' (μανία) and I would like to underline the 'sacred' connotations of the word here. And yet, independently of any 'companion', only the poem comes across, only the poem is read and measured against us.

Tassos Denegris

Death in Kaningos Square
(1975)

COLD WAR

Turn off the lights
secure the door
shut the windows
and turn on the station playing marches.

Hang black crepe on the walls
collect bread and make rusk
wholesale dealers have cornered the olive oil
and we'll eat the fish scales and all.

November 1952

SACRED WAY

Sections to the southwest
sections dressed in rags
smoky shapes shut the gates of the sky
sections to the southwest
sunset falling and they were
slashed on the breast of your
silence lunar rocks
sheets without corpses
stucco bricks earth
strewn at the door of your shame.

December 1952

WHITE HORSE

Hooves pounding sword points
cracks opening in the ground
groan diffusing in the air
measures light shuts down day
the anchors of a wounded ship
just like crosses placed on tombs.

April 1953

ELEGY FOR DEAD YOUTHS

Now here's the hardest thing of all:

Those who departed before they felt
the tree's joy watching itself grow
branches and leaves stretching day by day,
before dwelling in their own home, a quiet house by the sea.

Those who departed before they could
say what they would have wanted to
those whose thought was cut off
in the middle by the disease
that rots the flesh and spoils the blood
or those left behind in the deep ravines of Asia
without even a woman's touch upon their limbs consumed
those who led the way for six hundred moons
now have faces covered in thick cloud
and their deeds sleep in the land of lotus-eaters.

June 1953

EPITAPH

Flowers coffins and the damp
how bitter this organic salt
when the carriages wait for their passengers
in the circular square
and people must endure patiently
outside the ancient palace.

Flowers clouds thick books
twenty years scattered
on what was lost
and those who forced your hand
to your mouth now rub in sealing-
wax and stop all speech.

Flowers, cinema, thick books…

November 1953

DEATH OF AN OLD WOMAN WHO BECAME A NUN

I don't understand, I don't understand
only my heart is able to knock on the wooden door
there where the old woman, stopped clock on a white wall
awaits burial.

Just yesterday she gathered olives in her apron
the day before she fasted on the bread she didn't have
now her memory stands motionless as Lot's wife.

She can't even think of the consequences
when angels clad in black panoply
their hair entwined with the century plants
will bear her through salient spaces.

Brilliant narrow lane
prey of dogs
nun without a convent
malarial the dog of the pharmacist
I have no idea who will stand firm
when death swells
and guards change their lookout posts.

January 1954

PROCEDURE

Even this taxi but another of death's pretexts
cautiously speeding along the main avenue
the myopia of the other driver
coming up a side-street
doesn't recognize you, doesn't love you, bears you not the slightest hate
still it's another pretext of death
for you smoking so unsuspectingly in a dark cab.

This is the purest of absurdities
and its interpretation as obscure
as a Medieval Legal Document.

Wednesday 13 May 1959

THE EXAMPLE OF LEONARDOS

Leonardos at the age of ten
racing along on his bike
fell and scraped his knee.

He died in horrible pain
the disease is called tetanus
eight lines in the National Encyclopaedia.

Little Leonardos must have been very lonely
if one considers that his only friends
were his dead grandfather
whom he only knew about from tales
and that red bicycle of his.

Of the three only the bike remains
locked away in a dark storeroom
among photographs of wrestlers
and rusty fishing gear.

Saturday night, 27 June 1959

PERVERSITY

The crowd with the demeanor of eucalypti
and the immobility of statues.

People in uniform
and the spotlights of eight automobiles
scan the depth of the avenue
where the orbits of enormous shadows loom
and the cypresses touch the hide of the moon
sending a shiver through the galleries of the firmament.

No one understood what evil there occurred
they all escaped
even the butchered victim escaped, who knows how,
leaving only three or four fingers
and the fire-gutted house gone where no one knows.

Only the bathtub was left
and that foil
the lady on the fourth floor collected for the blind
or more accurately for the dog that guided the blind.

No one knows what evil there occurred
many ask themselves if any actually did
and continue to adopt the demeanor of statues…

1959

FOUR POEMS FOR ELENI

1

Of all the women on the island
the one missing was also the loveliest.

2

And if I held your head underwater
and if I tried to erase all traces
in a strange bed with new customs
it was because I loved you so
and was terrified
of you leaving me.

3

And the ape bent behind the doorknob
for a whole week under the lights
on the road to the hospital
silence, boards and workers' acetylene lamps
on the wounded sidewalks
on this road with those lights
a strange demonic look
in your eyes
I held fast to Eleni's flesh
that strange look
scaring me stiff.

4

Empty as the steppes
freed of bells and vegetation.

March 1961

LOUKIANOU STREET

The monkey dancing, decked out in crepe, with a harmonium
the mice in the swimming pool
like seaweed in the sea
the metal sheeting and the eagle
white moons left hanging
this mistrust overwhelms us
money contracts and hunting
stout wire so the sea
and the eagle will not escape.

Beauties themselves antiques
glass panes movements ancient victories
the solitude thick as is the fear
the beauties and the psychoses
photographs and hair-styles
record players voices the street.

Lie after lie in those eyes
here the nausea on side-streets
withered wreathes at entrances
printed matter and the concierge
behind the figure and the flesh
shadows on the walls silence in the parks
your face and the weather.

Night 5 July 1961

THE SPIES

I am not afraid of river currents, sleeplessness and blades
only the messengers
and the ladies under cover of baby carriages spying on you going by.

As for spiders I quake at their silent tread
and that metaphysical ability to stand on the ceiling
following my thought with a dark eye
without making even the slightest sound.

9 May 1962

THE EPILEPTIC'S DILEMMA

Whoever is able to walk in the rain
without getting his shadow wet
has God within him
Father Son and Holy Spirit
Burning swamp, The Crucified One and Pigeons of Nations
For all the others starvation, *tailleur*, birth control
photos of stars.

Looking chaos straight in the eye
vanity of Vanities
hung on your rage
waiting for the demon to emerge
for you to equate with the others
starvation, *tailleur*, photos of stars etc.

February or March 1963

SEX ON THE BRAIN

Suddenly this mania seethes within you
for war, rhythm, the sex act
the weather changed so suddenly
mild, the wind at half-mast, the power in the ground and plants.

The change reverses blood, shuts off rain
launches demonstrations, primitive festivals, revolts of native tribes.

Sex act linked to doomsday
neither in retinas
nor in film-clips
Diffused through your senses and your soul
along with doomsday
lasting for ten seconds, just like the final spasm.

13 September 1963

IOANNA

Waiting in the dark along the main streets
Sunday evening waiting
Sunday evening
Ioanna of August your tall silhouette out there waiting
I'm unable to get my mind
off your smooth round knees
while you are headed north.

Waiting for Saint Ioanna
Ioanna the whore
Ioanna my beloved, waiting to hear your familiar footfalls
Sunday Tuesday Wednesday
waiting in vain for Ioanna
Unable to abide the crowds
Former officials late friends infants beauties
deliberately confusing my thought
ASTIR Vouliagmeni Common Market
just so I won't think of
Ioanna half-naked in her dark pension.

13 September 1963

UNCONDITIONAL

It's a world emptied of you
mere fabrications all the rest
and subterfuges of the moment
the landscape
is called Mexico City
or the Tower of the Winds.

1963

CLOSE-UP*

I saw my beloved
in disagreeable passages
and priests, the vicars of God.

City police, the friend of my friend
Saturday nights
madness pocketed
I saw my beloved.

End of October 1963

* Title originally in English

EXTREME DESPAIR

Green door
studying the lights
children's bears who speak from their bellies.

Uprooted
despair
outcry
knife
threat
spectroscope slalom salt desert.

Studying the lights on the third floor.

18 November 1963

THE ASSASSINATION OF NIKEPHOROS FOKAS*

When the prince removed his iron armor
and asked to be baptized a Christian
the congregation then surrounded him threateningly after
    the baptism
and began to strike him in a rage
the prince remained solemn
trying to make out those he knew
who most probably were taking their revenge
but he was not able to see faces
because hate had transformed them into wheels
spinning at a vertiginous speed
thus did he remain staring vacantly

remembering most likely his childhood
on Deinokratous St. those large marbles color-swirled
in the shop-windows
Tourkovounia, Richard the Lion-Hearted
Loukia and perhaps things insoluble
insignificant to the reader.

Later the congregation from fatigue or tedium most likely
stopped smacking him around
and each of them returned
to his daily occupation
beauty salon the one, shareholder in a Company another
baseball players, tour guides, flower-sellers.
The prince forgotten, abandoned

left at the city fringes
next to the steel mill.

---

* Nikephoros Fokas: Byzantine Emperor from 963 to 969, famous for taking Crete back from the Arabs. Assassinated in his palace bedroom in 969.

Since then he's been wandering about smoking
in that grey tunic worn by the Air Force
indifferent to air pollution, elections,
relatives and the theatre
showing a particular preference
for VEGAS ice-cream and soccer matches
whether played on Sundays or Wednesdays.

The story is not imaginary
and has been preserved under the title "the Assassination of
    Nikephoros Fokas".

November 1963

VERDICT

Either balconies or street lights
a fait accompli
in a sealed envelope
at the whim of the mailman.

9 December 1963

HIGH AND DRY*

I knew that by sounds
and sounds alone I would reach the moon
the dark side of the moon
green
pale green
with the yellow bellies of the quarries
green
and thus as the sounds grew stronger
women and children and warriors
began arriving from all directions
clutching uprooted shrubs in their left hand
and wooden lances or goldfish in their right
to listen to and see the priest.

And as the sounds grew steadily more remote
sometimes the heavy tread of the tiger
on the blackened crops

sometimes a mathematical thought perfect
as a spider's web
and everything frozen
bells and icicles
then the spirit came down
to purify the hate
and we touched the green rind of the moon.

Saturday 8 February 1964

* Title originally in English

THE GENERALS

On the dark veranda the one covered by a wooden roof
supported on green columns
the generals were waiting saying not a word
and when the cry of the night-owl was heard
one of them ran into the green house
and all of them imagined the wireless had rung
or he'd been struck by an important idea
related to the troops battling
on the other side of the mountain
the general then returned with a cup of coffee.

The landscape was reminiscent of the Far East
the environs of Osaka
with the flowering almonds at the entrance
and one general thought he saw someone running
out past the mountain
the daughter of the director of the boarding-house
dressed in a new garment of white or praline-like beige
but it appears the other generals were seeing visions as well
for they were indifferent to the battle
rooted to the spot looking at the mountain and the gorgeous sunset.

Friday 25 March 1964

FAUST AND INDIAN CANNABIS

Peltasts, traps, slaked lime
white Siberian fur with whipped cream
warm lethargy
I don't understand a thing
I'm not lagging behind in anything
on the contrary I'm miles ahead
rarely has a man actually said go screw yourselves
to the collective values of the European spirit
comprehension, monuments, expediency, superiority
inferiority, Michelangelo, Bardot.
conversation, tutelage,
rarely
without giving in exchange
one square acre of his soul.

Saturday evening
I was an angel, bear, humble, powerful
apathetic
in chaos present everywhere
concentrated in a moth hole
or an echo.

April 1964

MY PARTICIPATION IN A SUCCESSFUL ROCKET LAUNCHING

We might have been riding bikes in the grass
lying down afterwards and gazing at the sun and the fence
or even achieving absolute serenity
opposite the neon lights and the lances
we may have been on the streets, at the barber shops, in the villas
mounted on proud ladies
you too could become One
looking for a pattern for women's clothes
counting the days
lingering in beds of lovers
shuddering herself at the shooting stars
in foreign cities and under bastard skies
in horror, isolation and terror
in dark dual-natured chambers
for intercourse, for sacrifice and then heading out
you too could become One
soaking like a crumb in water and paper in the damp
undoing the nets, hunting down the cobwebs
boundless after five childbirths
you too could become One
a steppe in Asia
perhaps in old mansions
the finger on the trigger
revolutionaries aiming at birds
will hit them in the head.

May 1964

EQUILIBRIUM IS MAINTAINED

Equilibrium is maintained thanks to the small child
walking straight as a ramrod in his green cloak
through the dark January afternoon.

BOSSA NOVA

Academy Street
Paradox Street
Police Street
Impunity Street
Descent into Hades Street
Suitable for Strolling Street
Bodiless Saints Street
complete with earth and corpses.

27 January 1966

TOWN PLANNING

White water
black water
sea bottom
arrangement of a lost city or
convoy.

The shadow of the settlement
and a human like a wing
vertical light
noon in Jericho.

10 October 1965

DEATH IN THE SQUARE

At such moments of irrational and otherworldly joy
when you can make out death while
others pass by unsuspectingly in Kaningos Square*
and death there right alongside them
where he's been transformed into a lottery seller
so insignificant there in a beige suit
a disabled person's rosette in his lapel
as soon as he realizes that no one
but no one suspects him
he transforms himself into a doorman.

I'm in a hurry now
to say what I saw there
this morning from the seventh floor.

Now I see how memorial services and forecasts were created
the usual sermonizing and time-tables
the well-off and the cowardly
habits forbearance bordellos
that is why no one
is able to make out
death
in Kaningos Square at 11 in the morning.

I got there in time for the final transformation
when dressed as a salesman he stood behind
a table
with red windmills
spinning as if possessed
at the slightest breeze.

---

* Kaningos Square: one of the main squares in downtown Athens.

In this strangest of joys
in this state where nerves don't obey the brain
and memory's out of joint and walks about freely
a tumbler at his aerial tricks
in this strangest of joys
with the body defeated by the selfsame tumbler
omnipotent and self-contained
you can clearly see into the damp prisons of a woman's desolation
can articulate the vertebrae of rhythm
and seize hold of death
helpless and cowardly
in its desire to avoid confrontation.

27 January 1966

LENT

The child's head unifies the space
adds dimensions to the freezing cold
snow doesn't suit this city.

A few murderers major trials
there are no victories
now with this snow.

The Vespa seized up in the garden
the woman in bed
on her back
the iron frame of the bed the outside border

The others
bankers, lepers, Charles, AEK*
a compact world
which calls on you to submit.

27 January 1966

---

* AEK: one of the main soccer teams in Athens

THE SLIVERS OF DAY

The time hasn't come yet
for the trees
to become one tree
the day looked grim
midday and the doors of the brilliantly
lighted drawing-room had yet to be opened
where the peacocks are waiting for
the awarding of the Oscars

courtesans wandered about with carafes
the day looked grim
and through a leaky cloud
a parachutist with a drum
smashed the air.

27 January 1966

THE CORONATION

The wolf froze in the deserted pasture of Et Quá*
gray stacks of hay
and the dogs' wind
portended storm.

With furry little kalpaks made of fox
they violently drag the orphan Ut*
toward the clearing
so they may anoint him sovereign.

31 March 1966

---

* Et Qoua, Ut: these names are the poet's invention

BALLAD FOR JANE FONDA

Flute water skiing
tarot intuition
on stairways
with wind
and darkness
in a Portuguese bed in the United Nations Building
outdoors on the Pnyx* or in Brittany
wherever
like the dog wherever I happen to find you.

Magical image
scholarship given to my erection
fox that roams the marshes.

26 September 1966

---

* Pnyx: gathering place during sessions of the People's Assembly. Later site of the "Sound and Light" performances.

KING'S PALACE HOTEL*

In any case this advertisement
for General Motors is a beauty
and those strange mechanisms made of nickel
like a magic ship three-storeys high
which setting off from the minor harbor of Kymi
will carry us to countries
with unique populations
Priscilla, Maria,
and the regimental colors
of Calvin Domitius†

17 May 1967

* Title originally in English
† Calvinus Domitius: a Roman Consul who commanded a center of the Legion at Pharsala, Greece in approximately 40BC.

GREECE, THE LAND OF MIRACLES

A choir of contractors builders
execute Handel's Requiem
Members of Parliament paint orchids
the general develops photographs of
The Virgin Mary in the darkroom.

This world was not made for us.

May 1967

UNNATURAL PROCEDURE

In the home of the deaf man
things were approaching the combustion point
the unnatural procedure
ceded its position to an unexpected tenderness.

In order to lessen the tension
in the home of the deaf man
they threw out the Frenchmen
his mother had written him clearly and carefully
about one of his brothers who was going
to become a priest
"Numskull. Does wearing a cassock make you a monk?"

The revival of the microbes
was achieved at the same time as death
and Adele not even knowing
what attitude to adapt
faced with this sudden ugliness.

May 1967

6

I must learn to like 6
up to now I've disliked it
just as I've disliked
Zurich and Hydra
however this March I have felt insecure
that's why it's time to declare
a truce with 6
I have to be on good terms with numbers
with numbers if nothing else
so I can have it out
with the Ides of March
so I will really try to like 6
with God's help.
I feel very insecure
and all I've gathered has been scattered to the winds.

18 March 1969

The Blood of the Wolf
(1978)

HE SPIRIT OF BOSSA NOVA

You advance in circles
descend
spiralling
hang hovering and the city
can't hold you
nor can any city
come to accept your harmony.

Your outfit the lightest green
your fingers dislocated
feathers of a peacock
your temperature an even 70.

Protect yourself
and never ever die
the Girl From Ipanema*
spirit of the air.

23 November 1969

---

* Ipanema: a wealthy district in Rio de Janeiro

MOMENTARY

Sailors talk about women
merchants about opportunities
billiard players put chalk on their cues
the captain recalls bad weather.

2 January 1970

PASSION AND WHERE IT LEADS ME

First I was attracted by your virtue
then I liked your thighs
later came your orgasms
like a swan caught in a dream
like a maenad.

Later I came to loathe your virtue
and forgot about you and your charms
Terra Firma of fish
psychotic Theodora.

January 1970

THE BLOOD OF THE WOLF

What are you looking for so tenaciously
the dog or your pills
what are you trying to find on those red BP maps?

Who knifed who
in which city were the headless cyclists found
if the Cyclops were still alive
he'd be wearing sunglasses
and if they were to awake – may it never happen – those who
died of leprosy
they would pay more attention
to their dress, and their appearance generally?

Who poisoned who
he who knows should tell us
who how and why
occasioned by the name of a lake
or Caballero Chewing Gum?

What are you looking for so tenaciously
on shelves in books in beds
in Chronos' hidden voices.
In unfamiliar glances.

The blood of the wolf will fall upon you
and the wind will eat your face
like a rodent.
Can't you see your struggle is in vain
the blood of the wolf, like I said, will fall upon you.

22 January 1970

MODUS VIVENDI

Which tenderness overflowed
like the bang of combustion
on undulating carpets
never before a woman's glance like hers
my sweet Theodora
you who should be living on hookahs and bonbons.

You're obsessed by IBM machines
the nightmare of the CIA
and only I who am writing the poem
only I have the desire for something better
the same desire that drove Simon Bolivar
E. Piaf and President Nixon
in this endless adventure
which for the first was a true triumph
for Piaf a stomach ulcer
and for Nixon something even worse than mere deprivation
a whole life spent far from cafes
women of loose morals and amusements.

22 January 1970

SIGNS AND WONDERS

The walls quaver like water on window-panes
and of these two doors before me
one is like the door of an elevator
which has just reached the ground floor and is about to open
and a gangster in a pink suit get off.

The other is like a door
to an inner corridor
which is usually kept shut
only opened to remove
on a gurney
the still anesthetized
patient who's
just been operated on.

Ophelia
in a red jumper
never stops laughing
would that her laughter
had something of the permanent.

16 March 1970

OSTRACISM

Who was it spoke of this from the garden
with its palm trees and wild pigeons
who will end up the convict
the roar of the crowd still fresh
so foully calling you
traitor and other names just as bad.

Not even nature was left you
for consolation or light.
The trees you so loved
as if they were your children
were removed from your sight
by iron bars and walls.

No one is safe
doors are hurriedly locked by
Senators and whores.

They wander through their thoughts
but the Law does not recognize
stumbling blocks and keyholes
passes straight through locked doors
as if it were disembodied or a laser or something
unbelievable, even more powerful than the imagination.

Lawless city
you immersed the metic's family
in shame
and multiplied your own
contradictions
like the eggs
of hideous bugs.

31 March 1970

JUDGMENT DAY

The sky will come crashing down one day
and the sea become a quarry
only the sun will remain, an orphan
and the earth a multi-storied morgue.

Saturday 2 May 1970

SPRING FEVER

Day after Easter and I was walking
along with Demetrius I, The Besieger*
or more likely his ghost
who got side-tracked
and instead of heading to his usual hangouts
landed on Lycabbetus†
on that night so luminous
peeking at
the couples embracing
and their sweet effusions.

26 May 1970

---

* Demetrius Poliorkitis (The Besieger): King of Macedonia 294–288n BCE. Fought many important campaigns in Greece including the famed siege of Rhodes from whence came his nickname, "The Besieger" (Poliorkitis).
† Lycabbetous: second large hill in Athens with a church at the summit and a magnificent view of the city.

DESPERADO AGAIN*

My soul a void
and uninvolved in public affairs
or hope-bearing messages.

17 July 1970

---

* Title originally in English

THE SCANDAL

Someone named Govil
a well-known madman in town
who used to go round in a gondola
with his dog who went by the same name.

So someone called Govil
exploiting his fame as a lunatic
went buck-naked
at noon and reveled
in orgies with his dog and friend.

The cooler-headed intervened
and scandal was avoided
the vilification of the patrician
came later and
the scandal broke out elsewhere.

The Chief
of Police, Captain Zambia
was found
or rather jointly found
not with a dog
but with his subordinate
named Serafino.

August 1970

TRAFFIC ACCIDENT

She went running break-neck
this mature lady punctual
in her appointments and in her thoughts
she was taken over by the downhill slope
under a cloud the relatives tagged along
to this final celebration of her coronation.

She hurried to catch the bus
without realizing what at the next step
what would happen to her, what she would find
they laid her breathless on the stretcher
concluding with crosses
and her tailored suit in the grave.

Beginning of October 1970

ANATHEMA

A curse on you and your tower
may landscapes and echoes shred your memory.

Anathema on you and your trees
may snakes and riddles coil round your reason.

A curse on you and your animals
may frogs nest in your pubis.

Anathema on you and your words
may horror and rags blanket your future.

December 1970

TYRANTS SHOULD BE AFRAID

Executioner demagogue
    foul DRAIN
of open-air sadism.

Light light-well
    latent DRAIN
of a multitude of surprises.

Practice putsch
    MINTING of currencies
cause of ambiguous corpses.

People sea of people
    SEA bitterly waved
supreme compassion.

2 December 1970

MASSACRE IN MY MIND

On the bridge a barrel
behind a landscape colored coralline
pyracanthus
and a sunset that bloodied doors.

May 1971

ANNOUNCEMENT

The more mendicants filling your courtyard
and the Man from UNCLE
and the forged educational patents
on the radio and so and so forth they will win out

Then you can be certain
you will suffer misfortune.
Your being will fall from its pedestal.

9 June 1971

ON SPRING

The place smelled of wild grass
they are grilling hare with oregano
in the outside world
and duty-bound in my sentry-box at the Pentagon*
I observe the spring
virgins of these environs as they go past.

9 June 1971

* Pentagon: the name the Greeks give the building housing the Defense Ministry in Athens.

ODE TO A PHOTOMODEL

Plastic woman
mineral water
blue and shallow

From all appearances happy
merry in any case
ignorant of Genghis Khan
knowing Mao only as a fashion statement
Paco Raban guides your thought.

Crucified on a blue Sunbeam
guardian of lawns
in the suburbs of counterfeit freedom
plastic crucified woman
everything will go just fine
provided it keeps going.

10 June 1971

KYRIE ELEISON

On the primary plane the day and its light
on the secondary the houses and their shadows
further back always that same mountain
and invisible to the eye
light out of the East
The Pantocrator.

October
Mercy
So I may climb
A little higher than the apes.

27 October 1971

WHAT I HAVE TO SAY ABOUT EMANCIPATION

Through the cracks in the rolling shutter
I see the house opposite in the light
the maniac cars of the city
it would be good if I were deaf.

I lie down to sleep in the tomb
I hear a bang in my dream
amid the movement out on the street
the royal tread of a puma.

He keeps tied to a chain
a young educated woman
they are passing the islet now
and to all appearances happy.

And I ask myself in my dream
what's emancipation and what's liberty
since she was given the chance
amid all the movement out on the street.

To escape once and for all
to go her own way
with her pack over her shoulder
by its silk strap.

And yet she preferred to remain
animal to animal, slave of the puma
smiling in the lava
and pleased by her super-mini.

28 October 1971

I DON'T KNOW WHAT TO SAY ANYMORE

I want to talk about the bonds
of spring
the torrent of refutation
the phantoms in the orifice of sleep
we in the mouth of the wolf
the river of womanhood
the river of hardihood.

This spring breaks bones
it breaks
and leads to the threshold of madness
for those who rely on
the sea
as a meaning, as water
as fantasy and glory.

I want to say the bonds
will become more tangible
intolerable is what they'll become
with the arrival of Attic spring.

22 November 1971

LILITH

This woman
was unable to sustain her myth.
self-seeking
fickle as the phases of the moon
with incredible cruelty
she stabbed one by one
the galloping consumptives in the sanatorium
and chose homosexuals
to hold the train of her bridal gown.

19 December 1971

THE SUN SETS AS WE APPROACH PATRAS

A red riverbed this sky
the dogs two-headed
the clouds at twilight
monstrous horses of the mind
and all the columns, stamens.

21 December 1971

THE SWEETNESS OF NIHILISM

I have the freedom of a nosedive
this dive
is mine alone
belongs to me.

27 May 1972

LEVELING

This person was a nobody
you beat him he beat you it was all the same
for him there were no motives
shifty and indolent
impudent and a voluptuary
he was a spineless
bastard
of good and evil
and the planet has filled
with his like.

29 May 1972

THE CONFUSION IS GENERAL

Everywhere lurks deep suspicion
like the heat that runs east to west
from Beijing to Brest
an autopsy everyone's precondition.

They ask how he died, the time
who was next to his bed
and with a wink and nod of the head
into a hammock they snugly recline.

They couldn't care less
who the dead man was
sometimes it must be confessed
the black dog is sadder than all the rest.

The world has lost all sense of a beat
the world kowtows to gold
mysticism traded for rice in a bowl
I want to wipe it from memory like dust.

9 June 1972

ΝΥΝ ΥΠΕΡ ΠΑΝΤΩΝ ΑΓΩΝ*

Horses at the track
people on platforms
those who compete
and those who just watch.

How I hate the spectators
who drink the blood
of athletes of actors
of mimes and horses.

Which is why if I were a horse
I would stamp on them
till there were no spectators
but only the contest left.

12 June 1972

---

* Νὺν Ὑπὲρ Πάντων Αγών: "Now the battle comes before all else"

PRISCILLA

With feminine sadism
she plunged the knife in his chest
there where the Stoa of Attalos* stands.

Ouzo was flowing in his blood
he felt power and turmoil flared and spread
Andronikos his name
son of an agronomist
his mother hid herself in the house
a church-hen and demented as well.

Andronikos, thunderstruck, mystified
stared as Priscilla
directed her knife
into him, in slow-motion.

For so many times he had done her favours
even treated her psychosis once
he had also had a child with her
two-headed
some
called it a monster and threw herrings at it
and others called it a two-headed eagle
with a certain destiny
in this vain world.

So he found it impossible to believe
that this Priscilla
standing here
had raised the knife.

White was the sky
with yellow stains
grass was sprouting between the paving stones

* Stoa of Attalos: part of the Athens Agora, houses the Agora Museum.

and the air smelled sweet
one could forget the corruption the malice
where the weather and this sweet aroma
were a double-edged knife.

With a strength not natural to his thin body
he tried to check the sharp descent of the knife
and like the hand he would finally lose in the *bras de fer*
he was able to resist
slowing the course of its descent
thus Andronikos
slowed motion itself

believing in the depths of his soul
that he was a spectator
at an outdoor event.

During that interval
that was a few seconds or as much as ninety years
Andronikos came to understand
he was involved with that scene in some way
and that he was threatened by the blade
but alas despite that in an instant
he lost that strength
that had checked the knife
like iron arms
or a harbor breakwater
which stops the topless
waves of the sea.

With the knife in his throat
he began to choke
lurched, fell
and in his delirium
said to himself in a whisper:

"The colors on the sign
are fading moment by moment
everything turning to sky and I am sinking

everything turning to sky
and is lost to me."

Portents swirled through his brain
foredobings of a minor hell.
"Sounds of Admiral Nava's
flotilla reach my ears
the neighs of battle
the clang of swords at Mediolanum*
the kilos I would lose
fighting the Iberians
in caves and gorges.

"What is this knife doing
in the top of my throat
as I slowly sink…"

Going deeper and deeper
a little more and he would slip away
and his fleeting soul
would take leave of me.

And thus he was abandoned
by Priscilla and by fate
all alone and unaided
straining to give up the ghost
like a cat, or a sinner.

And she disappeared
the memory of her lost
she withered and turned ashen
there on her farm
with the pigs the olive trees
and the expensive cutlery.

Andronikos went on to live after his death.

28 January 1974

* Mediolanum: the ancient name for present-day Milan.

Sulfur and Apotheosis
(1982)

THE FIRST MURDER OF THE CAT

Something exploded in the air
like a rag that caught fire
brown in the sun
the something that exploded
cat slaughtered
murdered by
professionals riding by
in Citroens with foreign plates.

Her battered head
traces out orbits
of despair
in a final spasm
the cat's body
jerked once
before it died on Alopekis St.

But the fault
lay with the city
because down deep
it never loved
the cat
before it died.

Fetishists felt a chill
and the zealots of freedom
occupied the entire allegory.

Get organized.

16 March 1970

SUNSET

The sky was all the best
there is in yellow
sulfur and apotheosis
it was yellow before it was named
color of hate
color of jealousy
color of madness
it was the flesh and the yolk of lightning
before there arrived the flags of the factions
the standards of kings
the rags of saints
it was the finest of our expectations.

This color
this yellow
disappeared from the face of the earth
wiped from History.

22 November 1971

NORTHERN SUBURBS

At this hour when the suburb
is sunk in its chloride sleep
rosebushes dripping on pitted earth
a few needles falling off the pines
on the roofs of cars
and the steaming street signs,
at this time when the minor
Lords of the day hang
suspended in repressive sleep,
this is the time when driven away
by the Bulgarian and enraged
with myself with the space
I discover completely by chance
that the suburb where she is sleeping
is dead and frozen solid.

I race to get out and make it
in time to see the foot of the hill
to find the Indian woman's stairway
and the loudhailer of the dead man
to do something anyway and escape.

20 December 1971

THE INTRUDER

Suddenly I found her there before me
her face like the moon
with those blue eyes of hers
eyes of celestial innocence
the Greta Garbo of refugees
the serene sunrise
I grew dizzy as a fly in the web
of an invisible spider
and like a madman
I thundered down the stairs.

During the heat-wave I was thinking of the Byzantine
sun-glasses covered her electric glance
like the Virgin Mary seated
begging
for mercy from her servants.

27 December 1971

THE RIVER

Now what's left?
The river; its current takes you aimlessly
through all the places you wished for
the landscapes of your soul.

Your soul has now turned icy
it's doubtful you can even see
the houses in the mist
the riotous flora
the cat slowly creeping through the cold fog.

Setting its own pace
the river takes you along with it
I lose sight of you and I can't understand
if I'm me
or you're you
which of us the one drowned.

15 July 1972

THE GREAT PARANOIAC

And he too is bluffing
everyone and everything
a paranoiac in a border
country
it couldn't be more incomprehensible.
The confusion that grips him
and this deep despair of his
lead him amid the darkest
shadows and dinosaurs.

He lives like a saint
reclusive
pleasures offend him
he makes the sign of the cross
you'd think he was mocking them.

Gods and demons both assisted him
and he bluffed them along
now they've abandoned him
and his fate has been cut off
from its umbilical cord.

So they think: He
lifted off one more
into the spaces of paranoia
and clutches vipers to his breast
and speaks with Essence.

21 August 1973

I LOVE PEACE BUT WHILE I AM SPEAKING THEY ARE PREPARING FOR WAR

We'll get embroiled in the fighting again
without ever wanting to
they provoke us and make fun of us
sneer at our customs
insult our minds.

We're surrounded on all sides
by their army swathed in lamé
their terrible symbols
superior not in firepower
but insolence and vulgarity.

We'll get embroiled in the fighting again
without ever wanting to
with no war material at all
our platoon leaders listen to music all day
and when it comes to food
greens herring and ice-cream on a stick
our morale in tatters
from the flu epidemic.

Their deranged squadrons are guided by remote control
and it is their own mind
that has got them worked up
the powerful loudspeakers
and the magic screen.

We'll get embroiled in the fighting again
ill-prepared, entangled
in the reins of our own horses
periods of torment followed by cooling off
with our heads in the clouds, confused.

Now the enemy has abandoned all pretext of shame and convention
they've put a stop to our music
they thrash the smallest
to put fear into the strongest
and keep them from talking back.

And suddenly from the depths
of our beings a cry
surged forth husky and hollow
like that of a wolf.

There was not a word of sense to it
not even a slogan
it was a cry charged with electricity
patience a thing of the past.

the mountains shuddered
the rivers froze
and we pounced on them…

When the sun awoke
and the day grew
their bodies were nowhere to be found

not even a trace
of their perfidious presence
left in the place.

And we go on living well
and will, in our own way
until things fall apart again
and the fighting starts over once more.

26 December 1973

THE LITTLE CONDOTTIERO*

The little condottiero
with his broken solar face
his arm motionless on the sheet
pinned there by the serum.

Heat wave
the neighbourhoods finished with tanks
the hills he wandered as a child.

There is puzzlement in his eyes
perhaps some fear deep inside
like an animal that's been beaten
he keeps an eye on his own blood.

The condottiero is little
and is obviously very sad
that is why he races back and forth
throwing punches reading comics
yearning to be of use.

What is he trying to forget
what premature passion drives him on
wagering everything and perhaps only loss
to gain giving himself free rein.

It's the contest, the sport
movement for him becomes escaping
his face a wound gaping
laughter brought up short.

30 December 1973

---

* Condottiero: from the Italian word condottiere word 'condottiere' which means warrior and refers to the professional soldiers in Italy during the 14th, 15th and 16th century.

PORTRAIT OF A KINDERGARTEN TEACHER

Elusive
compact and bestial
then elusive again
like a bird's wing or a vision
stock-breeder who sees
his mother dead these many years
her eye well-trained
poison instantaneous.

Emerging from the depths
emissary sent from Hades
witch of the Golden Horde
spawn of Tartars.

24 January 1974

THE PORTENT

Allegories come to mind
like that sudden illumination
in the sky over Houston
storm raging
hawk sizing up
its target and plummeting.

The airplane creaked
about to break you'd think
humankind brought to its knees
both it and its machine
in that time immemorial tempest
left to the ruling elements.

And suddenly I was overjoyed
at their plight
you'd think I wasn't one of them
you'd think their mortification
was my triumph.

And I saw so much more up there
in the lightning that cannot be forgotten
and which had no connection
with the miseries of this life
of idle expectations.

For one, I saw the wind
in all its omnipotence
and horses that were lost
as soon as you created
their image in your eye.
The clouds took on the shapes
of the goblins of allegory.

March I think it was
the message was given me
I was able to bring
its image to mind
to evoke at that moment
the spectre of hope
and so defeat time and weather
and withstand their dark.

Nevertheless I did forget it
the panic of the crowd
was now upon me
the mountains held me enclosed
and my way was lost
amid foreign portents
and idle expectations.

3 April 1974

OUTSIDE MY WINDOW

Outside my window
dirt collected in heaps
trash filled stairways
my kingdom subterranean
and my lover on the mattress
bed-ridden, ringed in snakes.

Her mind an arid steppe
where wolves walked for two months
her kingdom subterranean
the sea nothing but anguish, horror.

I look out of my window
the stairs and the sky
and the trash as I told you
and instead of a throne I have hay
and for food I have a hole.

Madness overwhelmed passion
the passion has not abated
ancient hates reawakened
and we sank into the depths.

In the depths densest darkness
the passion broken into three
the psychiatric clinics traps
and your mind in a well.

Somehow we must get out of the swamp
and somehow someone must survive
that one is you who have the arrow
as your symbol and emblems
now you must pay for your crime
and the unforgivable mistake
of hiding within your heart
so much life and such passion.

Holy Tuesday, 9 April 1974

THE TITLE IS DIFFICULT

As I move along the outer wall
of the reformatory
the spirit enters me
and somehow I unexpectedly penetrate
the secrets of the world.

Then nothing again
I'm back on the street
the trees bend before me
like ostriches
and I reflect how for just one
moment I touched
that permanent secret
those terrible ideas.

5 May 1974

MUSHROOM OF NIGHT

For you
mere speck in the snowstorm
I'm writing this poem
so the wind will carry it
on freezing evenings
to the plateaus of Asia
and you will remember
the years that lapsed
and left behind their wounds
miseries and triumphs.

So it's for you
and for the confusion you inspire.

29 April 1974

MY DEAD LEADER

There are times when my dead leader comes down
strange dragging noises and pauses made in rooms
as if he were looking around or trying
hard to remember
a point on a certain surface.

He moves in silence
he doesn't coerce, doesn't act, doesn't censure
he walks along with the sounds
insinuates himself into them and speaks to me
as he trails like a vapor through the house.

I know he came yesterday as well
vague and yet standing right next to me
encouraging me with this combination of sounds
the bond of blood that must contend
with the profound void of this world.

1 July 1974

LUCKY LUCIANO

No! I won't go into the deeds
I'm not a magistrate who might judge him
there is the Law of human affairs
and anyway he's
been dead for some time.

I just want to get a little of the atmosphere
there at Castellamare
to slip into the ambience of his mind
as the afternoon goes by
and the sky grows heavy
over the misbegotten balconies of Palermo.

To live if but for a moment
as if I were him
without any phony romanticism
that is without imbuing him
with a glamour he never had.

To get a grasp of the details
the myriad nuances
of his most deeply hidden thoughts
and above all else
the fury that possessed him
when he came to understand
no Organization is stronger than the State.

And how it was he got caught
between his innate antipathy
to organized groups
and that thirst of his for power.

I could be completely mistaken
it may not have been entanglement
but rather the thing itself
something you fear, hate
and in the end imitate.

Evening came down
and his soul mellowed
his life slid behind him
and skipped off like a deer.

It's not that I wanted to imbue him
with the slightest romantic tint
nor give his villainy
special consideration or a place
In History
just for a moment
to be inside his mind.

11 July 1974

INTERPRETATION OF THE POEM

Often the poem
has nothing to do
with recognition of worth, critiques
analysis and the like.

It has a chaotic past
a tremulous future
rosiest of horizons
unshakable foundations.

Often the poem
falls
like lightning on carts
scattering the horses into the forests terrified
while the drivers lose their ability to speak.

Like the genie they put in the jar
and it became smoke and escaped
thus the poem breaks
commitments and bonds
and you can't get a grip on it
with words and praise.

Slithering into bowels of the earth like a snake
it transforms the perishable
topples all the plots
Plutonian the poem and it has
not the slightest need for recognition
in chaos as it moves.

7 August 1974

POLYPHONIC

The trees stand before me
like judges hidden in the dark
from the open window I watch them and my heart
rejoices and pulsates.

The countryside seems to me like from another world
bizarre, inundating me with hallucinations
vultures squabbling and trees like I said
that look just like judges.

The day rolled past heavy as a tombstone
in the heat wave and with all the fires
which were lit on the edges of the city
by arsonists or those who had interests at stake

panic will soar high in the city sky
prices will rise just as high and our soul will crawl
on its belly in the dark
and nurse on mould.

24 July 1974

SOVEREIGN SKY

The lighthouse is gone, lost.
The bosom of the harbor laid waste
only the sunset remains
unchanged
by time and customs
identical with the cross
flaming with glory
and in the sling of the sky
the shadows of the mountain opposite
bent their bows.

6 January 1975

THE FOLIAGE OF FEAR

The trees spic-and-span
the cats stretched out
and timidly through
the foliage came the light of day.

The afternoons got shorter
and everything was so lovely
I got the idea of killing myself
because I can't bear

all this beauty around me
the sun on the wane
and the bitter discovery
that the weight of love

within me has shattered
the meaning of life.
Fear now is in command
if that be your wish.

27 January 1975

SELF-DEFENSE

When everyone pounces on you
like the dogs who maddened
by the silence of the night
bite whomever is at hand

keep a tight grip on your nerves
don't blow up and lose it
put your arms like a
collar around your head.

They'll run out of steam sometime
and will go back
to their oily villas
and their hollow families.

They have no God
no mercy recognize
and if you happen to be in their way
they push you aside.

The time of forbearance is past
the jackals are multiplying
and if you happen one time
to give them a whiff of blood

they'll come back in the silent
night and tear the roof
off your humble hut
and annihilate you.

Saturday night hit them hard
set fire to their house
so they'll suffocate in the smoke
and even their shadows be forgotten.

17 January 1975

THE FORGOTTEN BOAT

So I am the boat
that roams the lake like a phantom
night and day.

I loved the sea
it held me in thrall to its tempests
and its unbroken surface of water
like the brow of a dead man
really, I mean it, I loved it so.

But what do you expect of shipwrights
and even worse
are those who so providentially learned our secrets
and for our own good and to make some money
threw me into the lake.

So I am that boat
that has been waiting for years to compete
in the honorable tasks of the sea
instead of that
water lilies and other foliage keep me company
once in a while the moon as well
and who would ever imagine
that at the bottom of the lake lies in wait
the ghoul of love.

In this manner time has passed
and I am the boat that has been forgotten
night and day I wander about waiting
for great naval battles to come my way
– Trafalgar let's say or Actium –
that would grant me death in glory.

Because my life on the lake
may be a bed of roses
but there are no battles to take part in
and let's face it "I'm sick to death" of this vegetation
the beauty of the landscape has become an incubus
and as for love
like I already said it's a ghoul.

24 February 1975

BLACK THORN

Suddenly I saw it
a cat with its head in the garbage
and immediately an image was sketched out
emerging from the dark
dungeons of my psyche
which is that
mysterious
Atlantic
something flashed within me
a fervent joy
that I was an executioner
and the half-open lid on the garbage pail
a guillotine.

And can you imagine
them saying love is
guileless that it is
like the gladiolas
or like the infants who sail in their cradles
luminous rowboats across the sky.

30 March 1975

PIMP IN A PEOPLE'S COURT

I know what you're going to say:
That you were spoiled,
as a child they brought you
candy and caressed you
all those relatives who swaddled you royally
praising you to the skies on your name-day
carrying you in their fatty arms.

Now you tell me "my mother's
to blame for my misdeeds".
Those others who were orphaned
who would you like them to blame
for the disgraceful state into which they sank
the streets that vomited them out
or the reformatories?

Your mother was the commander
and you were the pet
but she didn't just emerge
from History either
her dwelling was behind the rocks
and her life spent with a rifle.

She was an Athenian
bricks and tiles
defined her mind
and a suppressed need to avenge
herself for that sorry father of yours
who abandoned her
buried in a miserable life.

So she is the one who raised you
cock amid tame beasts
and in the army
you made out just fine

bosom buddy with the sergeant major
and everything in apple-pie order.

When you were discharged
you took to loafing
and doing suspicious jobs
for 11 straight months
you studied card decks
how best to stack them
and how to mark the cards
how to divide up the hare
Before you cooked it.

You never once even tried
to sharpen your wits
to see where your spunk was taking you
and what your strength really was.
Now you blame it all on the madwoman
and play the innocent
who then am I supposed to feel sorry for
and who be unjust to?

You then are the typical example
of the ugliness
of this world
you are no Manson
the bad bird
you are not Ephialtes*.

You are the craven protector
the pimp as they say
and the informer
and your string of luck just came to end here.

16 May 1975

---

* Ephialtes: one of the sons of Poseidon by Iphimedia.

MUSIC CARRIED ME OFF

Music suddenly carried me off
to a treeless landscape;
snow everywhere
and there motionless in the middle of it
stood a woman
built there in the snow
fleshless
but still full of juice
to her right a bird
black as a crow.

The maiden of Time, I thought,
it seemed she was looking at me with favor
and perhaps with a smidgen of tenderness
but the judge on her right
confused me a little
infused me with awe.

Then everything vanished
while I reflected on
how miserable and slipshod your life had become.

4 June 1975

THE SECOND MURDER OF THE CAT

Heart-rending cries were heard
in the depths of night
vanguards of spring
flooded the streets
and the hospital's park.

A few moans
for a while
then quiet.

"That rattle, I think,
the final hint
or, an unidentified battle."
My hair stands on end.

The next day she was found
strangled
her murderer a dog
placid and undersized
obedient, on a leash.

His owner a foreigner
and perhaps by engaging in brainwashing
or slide projections
which showed cats devouring dogs
he drove the dog to murder.

Lawless city learn this now
there are many cats
difficult to keep track of
and finding them
impossible I would think the way they move around.

This craven murder
which you with your erudition embody
lawless city
with your plans to sow fear
you'll pay for that
beware
fear is a boomerang
the fear will enter you
and the cat your heart.

Iowa City, 21 September 1975

HER EYES

As the wind passes
and sets grass shivering
so am I jolted
as you pass by the door.

You disappear and reappear
you enter my brain
like the wells that draw
in the dark of the street

then who bends over to see
in their inexpressible water
the secrets that determine
gardens and swamps.

Her eyes encircle me
her eyes carry me off
her eyes forget me
and bring me to despair.

Everything looks hazy to me
the day laid waste
and I dream of you
at my feet slaughtered.

Later I change the dream
give you blood again
so you may continue to measure
the sea with lies.

Iowa City, 23 October 1975

SUNSET IN THE MIDWESTERN STATES

Along the border between two states
the Mississippi river and the sun
marshland in flames
the poet
wanting to transfer to paper
this lightning-like despair of God
for just a moment
to restore
the forgotten glory of the landscape
and the hope
which like the rich man's daughter
has been abducted.

Here at this river
that divides so many states
deep red purple and orange
are in a life and death showdown.

26 November 1975

IMPRESSIONS FROM A READING OF POEMS IN JAPANESE

Language of Asia straight from the larynx
violence all the way through
and vanity
unlike a cat
who sees the blemishes of life and people
the host of weaknesses
as stretched out on the tiles
it has a complete view
nor like that woman
the winter of '48
Civil War
raining frogs and planks
and the man's jacket tossed
over her face before its time.

Another sense of vanity
nothing sweet about it
death in advance
like the sword that suddenly strikes the shield
and smashes it
or shatters its point
—neither matters—
only the clash
of iron and that deep despair
this Asian tongue
conveys.
The trees stuck to the window panes
an army dressed in rags roaming about
proclaiming the victory of winter.

1 December 1975

ON THE POEM AGAIN

You don't know anything about the poem
it knows you
it functions for you and lives without you
the poem lives
without anyone and for everyone.

I can't go into details
and listen closely
to what I'm saying only if you want to
but be afraid
of the poem
if you can't love it
and even if you do love it
don't nourish the hope it will love you back
because the poem
makes others love
or be tormented or revolt
while it
flies off like an eagle at dawn
and disappears.

18 December 1975

PATRIOTISM

So it is comforting
that Sirkouf the dog
prefers me
to the Dutchman.

For despite the fact they gave him a foreign name
he smells of Greek grass
fights with the local cats
and distinguishes without difficulty
the local friend from the foreign master.

So it's comforting
that the dogs
linked to the smells of a place
remain
patriots in other words
in these difficult times
these polluted days.

6 April 1976

NOT TO MINCE WORDS

The foreigner is always a foreigner
don't forget that
even the one
who came on like a friend
palming off on you the most frightful platitudes
about the weather, the wine
the beauty of the land

keep him at a distance
don't fall into his trap
no matter how good appeared
his intentions, how accessible.
don't forget
in his briefcase
he may also be bringing you
a model of a prison with fans.

6 April 1976

IN THE SKY

The clouds
Japanese who remind me of aviators
kneeling before their emperor
as I fly eighteen thousand feet
above them from Denver to Chicago.

So love the airplane
and pray for it
in the sky.

12 September 1976

NATIONAL DEPRESSION

The black plastic
garbage bags
like two old ladies
sitting against a wall
or looking like a couple of nuns
fading into darkness
snakes all around hissing
foreign agents
and local provocateurs
and all of it hideous, not one slit of light in the dark
in this wretched assembly
only now and then
a remote explosion
as if something lifeless and heavy were falling into a well.

12 September 1976

TORTURE OF A CITIZEN WITHOUT ANY DETAILS

Sergeants inspect you
like a weapon from '48
like a cloudless landscape
as if you were incongruous
sergeants bayonet you.

23 November 1976

CONFIDENCES

The best poems
I heard in my mind
suddenly as they fell there
usually at night it was.

I wasn't thinking, just looking at
the friendships of trees
or the cat crossing
the road benumbed.

They entered me soundlessly
I was in a coma
with my eyes wide-open
like goblins.

But when I was sitting
at the paper ready to write
I was like a blind man they give a
thread to, to find his way out

or like I was a hand-picked
marksman and for a target
they gave me a shadow
to cut to shreds.

N. Heraklion, 21–22 November 1976

IMAGES FROM AN EXCURSION

        Boeotia
The poplars present arms
as we pass by at high speed
above the lake that became a meadow
and instead of rowboats and caiques
A chrome-plated tractor lumbers by.

        Pelion
Bare branch
like the string of a violin broken
in the air
and the dogma of the glory of the open sea.
Polyhedral landscape
the Aegean to the right
and to the left
Mountains rising up, martial songs
there amid a green majority
yellow plane trees
and chestnuts with leaves of copper.
Hallelujah.

12 December 1976

COSMOGONY

So when on the evening after
Christmas day
with those hideous electric lights along the street
I was observing people
far-off images came to mind
images and sounds.

Basin cistern crucible
crater of a volcano
the region a tangle of snakes.

Horizontal movement
fixed in chaos
mussels and Tyrannosauruses
cracks in rocks and all the time
the others keep coming:

The caste
the grazing and hunting
the bull's horns and the crown
the idyll in the forest
the fame of the horse
the tumult of the slaughter
the monarchy of passion
the first laws that fell
from heaven
the various appeals
to the king to the president
to humanity, ethos, religion
and the others keep coming.

People seem like bad copies to me
not real
not truly responsible
for their evil fate
as they go back and forth

among the fir trees left on the street
even paler than the electric lights
which piteously illuminate
the evening following Christmas Day.

October 1972

Instantaneously
(1985)

OCTOBER

The clouds white
cactuses before me
unfinished three-storey buildings behind
a tenth of the city submerged
in the depths of fog
this first Sunday in October.

Thin the light
nary a gleam
everything solidified in an instant
like a battle had ended
and a decision already handed down
as to who won
and who is now dead
and who will not be afraid of a single fear.

A little girl with a bike
moves without haste on foot
along the pavement
she'll be pushing
the bike uphill forever I think
since on the second Sunday in October
it happens to be her turn
to be the only motion
amid immobility.

How can I make this landscape a poem
as cheap-gun words are sniping at me
to the left and over by the quarries
the first prisons of Lykaones
emerge up ahead.
Behind them come children
Women holding them by the hand.

Equivocal image
will they fight
or are they looking for a little plot to take a stand on
at the boundaries of Filothei,*
and what will the locals do
will they take it amiss at losing
even a ¼ of their land
and in terms of aesthetics
will the mere sight of
these people here disturb them?

So the third Sunday in October
the sun enters Scorpio
and the terrible process begins
of transformation in Nature
and, at a slower rate,
in history.

14 January 1977

---

* Filothei: well-to-do neighbourhood in north Athens near the center.

LOS ANGELES

And I was expecting to find
the classic psychopath
aiming from high up
at unsuspecting passersby
who his split mind had confused
with his mean mother
like in films.

Instead of that
a bunch of cacti
complicated interchanges
and finally the fog
that slid into Malibu
and climbed the hills
like a leper.

Help.

4 March 1977

POSTWAR*

Just as in the old days
in the spurious forest
like a cat that's been stepped on
and nothing but despair
which can't cope in any
other way with power
popping up like a sheet of metal
and biting the potentate

yesterday as well
paper swirling and slapping trees
in the roar of the wind
I cried out in a rage you don't exist.

Today I feel differently
like night and day
a diffuse tenderness
drifts through the air
with plenty inside me to spare.

I open the window
carriages with six horses
pass before me
suddenly they pull to a stop
at the door of an inn
women get out

I see them lifting
their skirts gracefully
their laughter comes rolling along
like a child's ball on the shady verandas
of a fairy tale.

* Title originally in English

Then once more nothing
the boring landscape
dossiers and blank faces
and I'm still wondering
what could have caused
my sudden rising
for a moment into the air.

15 March 1977

INSTANTANEOUS

Out of side-street in Gyzi*
the son of the late Prime Minister
slipped out
mad
at least that's what they said
and me
endless misfortune
flat broke.

10 June 1977

---

* Gyzi: area of Athens where refugees from Asia Minor lived in the 1920s.

NEW ORLEANS

Under the light that drenches
Tulane Street
a terrible cry
bursts from someone
its dark cause remaining
a mystery:
Is this the howl of nervous collapse
or voodoo
from someone who was paid for it.

20 June 1977

THE BRIGHT IDEA

To take myself out of the middle and observe them
and suppress any
dealing I had with them.

December 1977

INVITATION FOR POLO

So when will we
gallop
picking the heads of the money-changers
as if they were daisies?

I'm talking to you.

December 1977

DESCENDING

And I who should have
done this and that
sometimes, I've practically
given up hope
falling victim to a maddening illness
my bones
all gone completely haywire.

Outside, an unusual winter
and the landscape
just the way my imagination wants it:
colored grey
two figures pacing from wall to wall
my father
hunting in Euboea
and me a child of five with the cartridges.

8 March 1978

RITUAL

Yesterday I flayed my hide
and flooded the place with blood
but now with this moon
I ascend higher
than even the satellites
keeping an eye on us.

1978

SAINT JOHN RENDIS

The mood of the day ambiguous
great plans in mind
but a feeling of vague melancholy
the working-class houses ochre
breathless balconies dotting the green
and what brings everything good
through its nipples
now blowing its top in the dust.

Three palm trees off to one side
stand as if impoverished
holding komboloi*
as a funeral passes before them.

Its charm
which comes and goes
with the wind
is now being tested by the trash
and the abandoned factories.

15 January 1979

---

* Komboloi: Greek "worry-beads", similar to rosary in construction.

SEPTEMBER MOON

Red half moon
to the southwest
I see on a balcony
three apostles
in their green robes
of cotton
squatting on their heels
sneaky, so they won't be seen behind the parapet,
as if they were cold
or were afraid.

But to the right
Tourkovounia*
a camel there in the dark
a shape patience might take.

The one image does not ruin
the other nor even annul it
opposite each they are united
into something truly novel
what the poem presents
the apostles and our hills as one.

15 January 1979

---

* Tourkovounia: series of hills in the suburb of Psychiko.

THE UGLINESS OF A DAY

The sky filled with sulfur
at two in the afternoon
it was as if it were night
the yellow electric reflected
in car windows
the despair of the world.
And here in a nearby suburb
I see poles rather than trees
and the fields taken over by building sites.

Such an ugly rain
cages and tears
no matter how you look at it
everything is nearing an end.

1 February 1979

THE GHOUL

I knew that your race
from deep in the past
was rooted in the rocks
and I said
you would have the power of an
Archangel.

It wasn't like that.
It's only at night you acquire
your own being
impose yourself through
your motions
repetition
memorizing by heart
in an obsessive ritual and thus perfecting yourself.

You live in unrelieved darkness
and the furniture in the house
like the cats in the dark
is lurking there
you living that lie
always the same stories
like

showing
photographs of women who for years now
have held high like a banner
family, race
while all around
foreigners were concocting invasions
peculiar languages
wounding the air.

You liked the lights
the electrified loudspeakers right till the end
and on mocking
the weakness of others
you based
your strange power
which spread its spidery webs.

Until

an entire mechanism
fell on you like a guillotine
and sent your head flying off.

4 March 1979

SUMMER SUMMARY

I carried on my shoulders the dogma,
July was familial,
and her mind ruined
by the heat wave, the intrigues
and the small recompense.

The fires destroyed the forests
the Greeks in confusion and discomfort
the Parthenon sick as a dog
and the new crusaders
ravaged the country where the weather was always good.

The end of summer came
in the sky great variety
and like wind in the windlessness
Of Ippokratous Str., Juantorena
Runs across small screens.

VENCEREMOS.

6 March 1979

THE WIND BRINGS

The wind has the smell of
People's Courts
and from far away
the sound of a harmonica
in the misty landscape
ghosts nettles
like snakes bewitched
stir.

23 August 1979

THE SAME OTHERWISE

The wind smelled of
People's Courts
and from the depths could be heard
the sound of a harmonica
in the misty landscape
and the nettles phantoms
like snakes stir.

27 August 1979

COUNTDOWN

Just like the grass
will punish the one who corrupted it
the animal with its venom will strike
the consumer
and the burnt forests
will come and cut off
your breath.

And you all unsuspecting
in your mobile iron scrap.

26 August 1979

INMOST

I'm running constantly and getting nowhere
never reach anywhere in time
nor do I ever pass anyone.

May I never catch up with anything
never pass anything, ever.

I want to run.

24 September 1979

THE EVOLUTION OF THE LANDSCAPE

The Thriasian Plain used to be here
all olive trees and Mysteries
now they've been fired from the technological landscape
of Eleusis.*

Flaming tongues, incomprehensible stations
tubing, canopies
a triumph so cool, composed.

The sea, however,
is not taking part
and has grown angry
because the pollution
has reached its organs,
those most intimate.

24 October 1979

---

* Eleusis: a town 23 kilometers outside Athens. During antiquity it belonged to Athens and was a religious center famed for its temple to Demeter and the Mysteries of Eleusis in honor of Demeter and her daughter Persephone. Today it is an industrial town heavily polluted.

THE SHOWDOWN

Your truth
and mine, so far apart,
two pedestrians face to face.

Your point of view
on my truth
and my point of view
on yours
two knights hacking themselves to bits
with swords and axes.

When deep in the night
roosters crow
the room soaked in blood
the truth long fled.

3 November 1979

UNTITLED

For the orphans,
for the orphans of psychosis and mistake,
for the orphans of the wind
and road accidents,
for the orphans on frontiers
and for those in large cities
in streams with frogs,
for the orphans of no moment
and for those worth noting
those who play in groups
in the parentheses of a whistle,
for the orphans of love
and for their dark dignity,
for the orphans,
for their endless glory.
Look at their radiance
in the mud.

4 November 1979

A DAY

The five-year old girl
who is talking to me about fear
and how she spent yesterday
focused on recollections:
the even younger boy who bit her
instead of saying good evening
the dog, the girl,
that other guy with the beard.

She brings harmony
into the dark room
and those recollections
from days I do not want to remember
have drawn me back.

The days have got much shorter
the light in its death-throes
on the window pane
and through the half-open curtains I see
the flags of autumn.

Don't be afraid.

23 January 1980

HORRIFIC CONFIRMATION

It's easy now for
me to make out
the plot.
This plot is
of multiple women's braids.
Foreign hands braid them and even more foreign,
multinational minds, almost otherworldly,
plan what's to be done with them.

There is sacrilege here:
tombs were pillaged and the dead exhumed,
in order to acquire them.
There is also robbery:
these were not their own women's braids,
they stole them.
There is – the most important –
an expediency that kills
because with these braids
the dark minds
will entangle everything.

17 December 1979

THE OTHER VERSION

I was thinking about Casanova
an old man
hurrying into the mess-hall
his once
neatly powdered hair
streaming in the wind.

He knows none of the fame
that would come down to us
and he takes no pleasure at all
from his old life.

Why are we so quick to draw conclusions
about a life we read of only in books?
I see him wipe his mess-tin with his bread
and he's unshaven
in someplace cloudy like Zagreb
or Trieste.

As for those stories
you tell me about Casanova
I have no idea.

23 January 1980

ELOQUENT PUZZLEMENT

Why does the June light
cloud memories and obscure
persistent ambitions?

Why so much unhappiness
seven-thirty eight in the evening
as nature ascends?

Because I, like the others,
vulnerable to wooden idols and delusion
fight back.

15 July 1980

CHRYSOSTOMOS SMYRNIS STREET

It's a pretty street outside my house
evening at the end of August
short row of trees
bricks permanently left behind
at the building site next door
and at the far end of the street
the light of a lamp is burning
the singer on the small screen
with a phallic microphone in her hand
going up and down
as the neighbors mechanically
watch the program
with the sound off.

End of August 1980

THE BEGINNING OF AUTUMN

Suddenly
an invisible axe splits it :
light and darkness.

The day is cut in two.

29 January 1981

THE MAGICAL PROCEDURE

So overwhelming in her uniqueness
she paints flowers on a trunk
in her grey light.
Without even thinking, she stares
for a long time and what she sees
does not exist for the rest of us.
Then she bends down close to
the wooden surface
her hand held close to her body
and puts in birds and makes lakes
landscapes from life and memory
entering there for a while she forgets herself
in the magical procedure.
And when it's just past midnight
she looks at her handiwork
not one bird is flying
nor do the water lilies move
the dream flew away and is gone.

30 January 1981

THE BARONS OF THE HOSPITALS

They stride around like Teutonic Knights
erect, their eyes fixed
on some far-off point,
followed by two or three others
who appear to have once held a shield
but are now holding a tablet and pencil
and throwing a curt glance
at the fever chart hanging
on the iron frame of the bed
as they invade the wards of the patients
and there is a stir
yet they pay no attention
as if they hadn't come for the patients
but for some ritual unknown to us.

They leave just the way they came
hastily and with their eyes fixed
on some invisible point.
Their assistants scurrying along
behind them like monkeys
while women with varicose veins
lie in wait at the corners
for a word with them
but they go right on by
as if they were signs marking the kilometers
and forge ahead lost in another world…

Where does their power come from
and who was it portioned out the fiefs?

December 1981

STABLE POINT

The phone call
like a visit
the old man sits
and waits.

30 November 1982

CHILD'S POEM

Bitter orange and
lemon trees and the sun
toss down gold coins
into their shadows.

The dark wins
night has fallen
and the trees fade
from our vision.

An accessible world
to spirits, to snakes
the scales tilted
toward the side of fear.

Again tomorrow
in the middle of midday
lemon and bitter orange trees
the sun king.

With the ducks the cats
the erect roosters
we became acquainted
and made many friends.

We will not forget you
magical garden
when at night you become
whatever we might imagine.

30 November 1982

DISAGREEABLE POEM

Horror piled on horror in the photograph
in today's paper
something even worse
than cannibals
because they believe some good may come
from doing such an appalling thing.

While here
on the National Road on the way to Lamia*
as I read in the caption
these pieces of scrap
dismembered a lot of people.

And putting their pain aside
as it would be spurious
since I don't even know them
I only mention it to you
because of all the horror
that managed to be piled
into a single photograph.

11 February 1983

---

* Lamia: the principal town in central Greece.

The State of Things
(1989)

THE STATE OF THINGS

Some would like to shoe me like a horse
indeed they brought
along the tools of music
to drown out
the banging of hammers.

And I am filled with clouds ;
caught in this dilemma
my purpose has been impoverished.

2 August 1981

BLURRED PHOTOGRAPH

They are combing his hair in the open air
he is clapping his hands
and you are shocked.

It's ivy gone crazy
he's afraid of the wind
he'd like to be straw
and be done with it.

It is the clearing
that was plowed
by the lightning
and you were spared.

He's the one who catches the wind
in the palms of his hands
he is your mirror
don't throw it away.

15 October 1981

VIEW FROM THE WINDOW

I look out the window
at the yard next door
when suddenly amid the grey
two brilliant reds.
A robin stands on a wire and gazes
at a red wooden cat
a toy forgotten there
sometime in the past.

Is it moved by fear or curiosity?
We get no answer
the apricot tree has withered
in this graceless place
which is suddenly set aflame
by this robin.

Good Friday 1981

LIGHTNING BOLTS

Like turbines
like nerves
or like the palms of the hands
horrifying in
their speed
as they inscribe
on the sky
electric midnight diagrams
in the merest wisp of time.

Their beauty
has no end
a shudder passes straight through out body.

27 September 1982

UGLINESS OF CIVILIZATION

Darkness fell.
my voice
a pilot just shot.

Then again
another
new scene
near the sea
Late Renaissance
plectrum
feasts boiling over
preparing a vast deception.

October 1982

UNCOMMON SNOW

Thus comes a day of joy a
day with snow
incomparable
like for example the one today

where the dark green of the trees
is not abandoned
to a merciless
white rage

say you're blind
and let the cold
lead you around
like a St. Bernard

to a better view
than the one offered
by our anarchic
capitalist society.

March 1983

BLUNTLY

The word an orphan with no father
gives way to delusion
or the mailman driven
to treacherous pursuits.

The word an orphan with no mother
it is sleek
you may well admire it
but it's heartless
and shows no mercy
and has never even had a whiff of
love.

25 August 1984

ZEN

So let's surrender
to emotions more ill-defined
to a stroll through the sky.

Clouds stationary and self-contained
do not foreshadow anything
but rather promise and affirm
a day that started with smog
stress, self-interest, compromise
perhaps will end
in an absorption with nowhere
with the head
of the Black Beast
who for your sake
was transformed
into a household pet
smiling at you.

29 August 1983

EASTERN VIEW

Squalor, wintry weather
I follow Evaristo Carriego*
from the room I'm writing in
as if by his side
maybe I'll be able to grab him
and bring him into our language.

At some point I get tired
turn my eyes to the glassed-in porch
see the back of the neighboring
apartment building.

Such wretched balconies
with their displays:
dust rags, garlic in a net bag
a wicker armchair
an iron crib.

Still further back I can imagine
similar constructions
until later
Mesogeion St.'s reached
boulevard of microbes
the terminal point
of that seductive mountain,
called Hymettus†
symbol of freedom to
me as a child.

25 September

---

* Evaristo Carriego: an Argentine poet, also the title of an essay written by Borges in 1930.
† Hymettus: principal mountain mass lying east of Athens.

AYIA MARINA, ATTICA

Geraniums black railings
and the spider spinning its web
high in the sky.

The sea before me
continually changes color
depending on the weather
the time of day.

An island that looks like a fake,
an island in a manner of speaking
off to my left.
It's child of the mainland
who's been weaned.

In the meantime night has fallen.
Suzukis and Toyotas
return to the capital.
Which is also why rows of lights
stigmatize the hills.

18 January 1985

ESSENCE OF THE LANDSCAPE

In this helplessness of the poet
who has caught
the beauty of the landscape
in its entirety
but isn't able
or just doesn't want
to convey it in words
to your mind and your heart,
there is a certain grandeur.

He triumphed over
illusion, which is
what makes
every poet want to
fragment Essence
so exaltation may benefit.

Glory to red
honor to yellow
giving everything they've got
the moment the sun
hides from our eyes.

18 January 1985

AFTER A SUDDEN RAIN

After a sudden April rain
the green of the leaves dazzles me
burnished and new born.

The abandoned garden
as if by magic
gleamed.

In the house
young and old
are watching animated cartoons
while the skinny
grape-arbor looms
against the glassed-in porch
and makes things difficult,
as their imagination is insulted
watching
the television program unfold.

I will carry on with my work
encouraged.

27 October 1985

SPARK

Is our perception more powerful
or the rag
which has gone mad and sailed off in the wind?

I was thinking about that
greatly discouraged
as I walked along a street
without a plot.

January 1986

DEAD END

The words lost their gait
and flounder.
The horrible hedge gloats.

What am I doing here?

27 February 1986

CONFESSION

My master is a doctor
my mistress is his wife;
there is a wolfhound as well
they love like crazy.

They won't let me eat with him.

March 1986

TWO BIRCH-TREES CONVERSE

This Slav
who believed in the divine
unexploited
fragment of humankind
why did he go off to die
in the city of calligraphy
and nightmare?

He went to unburden
his soul for a while
to get back
to the mystic life
where the smallest puddle
can become a homeland.

14 September 1986

31 DECEMBER 1985

Ultimate night
of December
where everything has
stuck to the window

I would like to set down
in an image
it's the mercilessness
of time that I want.

If I give it depth
it will be false,
the eye wanders
and is lost.

Pitch black
hides everything
the jasmine
All that's left

which stands out
in the night
just like that
white balcony

like the ship
all its lights on
at the dock
so proud.

Like anonymous
religious paintings
this poem has
no depth.

1986

AEGINA

Outside winter
it's cold and in the field
the pistachio trees are in torment
but
in the house
the music burning in the fireplace
is a wind instrument that refers to the universe.

28 January 1989

DEMATERIALIZATION

He should come closer
or perhaps leave
as usual
since he knows
that the rarest
feelings
come from
where realization
is not ventured.

14 April 1987

THE PICTURE BLOOMS

The picture blooms
when
the viewer instead of merely looking
probes deeper
and reveals need

which is what obliged the young painter
to make the painting
that is blooming here
as it awakens powerful emotions
which it seems bear no relation to the theme.

15 December 1987

BITTER CONFIRMATION

It is through this ordeal
are forged
all those who must
transcend fear
and view the world
from on high
that world
where at one and the same time
they live and flounder.

9 February 1988

DUBLIN

A caique turned over, half-sunken there
on the jetty at Howth
Excalibur SO 69 its name
and the rest of the particulars
painted a cobalt green
the wood of the hull
prey to the sea
which chews it up with small grunts.

But the mast
cares not in the least
about the water
that has settled in here
because it
will answer only
to the sky
to the sky alone give in.

31 August 1988

The Spirit of Defense
(1999)

TWO SKETCHES ON MADNESS

Let us suppose that we haven't reached
that black impasse, the abyss of the mind;
let us suppose that the forests arrived
with the imperial equipment of morning's
triumph, with birds, with the light of the sky
and with the sun wherever it happens through.

Kostas Karyiotakis (Satires)

I AM SOMETHING INCONCEIVABLE

I am something inconceivable
to the eye of man
I bide my time
as I have said elsewhere
at the great crossings
or with just one glance
I eliminate
fear and disastrous hesitation.
I know the uniqueness
of my mission
I help my neighbor
I uncover illusion
I battle impudence and vacillation
– The criteria are not clear
more frequently, the voice of instinct –
I take refuge in the clouds
how they alter their color at sunset.

The seasons change
in the length of a day
and there is no time left at all
for the soul to enjoy
or simply to suffer winter.

Mud dome of warm air
strong and solitary
which peak what depth
a trireme
barks in the night.

(Originally written 31 October 1971; this version from 1997)

I WAS STRUGGLING TO EXPEL

I was struggling to expel madness
which arrives in waves
as soon as it spots
coincidences favoring it.

Invisible are the conditions which create
the desire for dissolution
ocean
Kingdom of an autonomous plot
motion within motion
and scaly.

I was lying in wait in the tunnel
the water right up to my waist
and the mold an impenetrable barrier
thick dark, difficult
practically impossible for it to recognize me
lightning must strike.

The first responsibility comes
as if it were a storm
the heart a leaf that trembles
and it's trembling.

She surrenders to routine and dreams
of a carriage crossing
the Black Forest
uneasy stags
lie in ambush
and presences
I do not intend
to number.
The past is imposed
transformed
into a household pet.

The door of the elevator opens
onto the corridor of that floor
and most distinctly are heard
the mother's hooves.

I do not want to enter her knitting.

1973

EPITAPH FOR THE HATED MURDERER DUFT*

At the shooting range of Ai-Yannis
they are shooting the foreign murderer
just before the sun rises
a rainy day with a dense fog.

Not one tear will gleam in an eye
a sob would cloud the mind
dark as a cave his form
remote as a mountains' shadow.

He refused to have his eyes covered
he stood straight before the post
the bullets pierced his chest
and he dispersed like a cloud of dust.

Money was not his motive
murder and longing his aim
and as I'm writing this poem
the steam is still fresh

from this murky story
from such a fateful slaughter
from the blood shed wantonly
and the outcry from the world.

Quite a few would argue with me
they think I'm praising this murderer
that I'm completely at a loss
or I'm being thrashed by ghastly heartlessness.

---

* Duft: German, murdered several people in Greece in the late Sixties and came to be the last person executed in Greece.

But I must clear up for them
that the narthex of the poet
is the space found behind
the mind's eye and ear.

It is the other side of things
invisible to the judge
a drop of compassion and love
to the mad murderer and thief.

All that blood and again not enough
they shot Duft the murderer
on the shooting range at Ai-Yannis
raining and dense fog.

7 March 1979

THE STRAW IN THE DARKNESS

The straw in the darkness
does not exist for you
but for itself
remains what it is
and someone must open
the fanlight a crack
if just for a while
so the straw can gleam
like straw does in sun.

30 December 1988

IN PRAISE OF THE MOON

Summer has poached on
others' preserves
and doesn't want to leave.

And when I enter the cross-streets
on my left I see the moon
wrapped in a small
rainbow
still lacking that something that will make it full.

Her beauty
though in a minor key
is indescribable
like that woman
who glows from within.

October 1981

PERAMA*

There's the mountain
we came up
suddenly there before us
on the high school

excursion.
Treeless, rocks
all one emotion
end of the earth.

A landscape
of horror, and you know
it's been haunted
by the swelling

of the corpses
of the Asians
from the naval battle
of Salamis

3 October 1991

---

* Perama: port near Piraeus directly across the island of Salamis.

THE TRAUMA HOSPITAL

Ambulances
continually arriving
and the policemen
don't have time to write things down.

I am on the second floor
two women come out
of the operating room
the pain of one of them
more resonant
my child, she cries
visitors freeze.

I'm running up the stairs to the fourth floor
trying to get there fast
my aunt has slipped and fallen
as she was crossing the street
right next to the Pentagon
and broken something
at the age of 86.

In the first three wards
young people
and their motorcycles
suffocate in their plaster
while they're kept company by parents
and cheerful girls with transistors.
Among them the extremely old
shuffle by with their drips.

There in the kingdom
of ailment
a woman
young and beautiful
by the door

of the elevator
resembles a wind-up toy car
in a landscape that's been gouged out
by napalm bombs.

Holy Thursday and doctors
and nurses are getting ready
for the holiday.
From the waiting room on the fourth floor
I watch the sun setting
Over Pefki, Neo Herakleio
and the meager olive groves.

Down at the exit
a sergeant of the gendarmerie
is talking to two women
and rather hesitantly
gives a man's shoe
to the eldest.

I leave the hospital.
Spring's dictatorship
rules the gardens, the air
no correspondence at all
with the gloominess I saw
beauty is lurking
makes the pain hard to bear
but in nature, innocence prevails
and evil
has put down no roots there.

13 October 1985

THE HEAT WAVE OF 1987

Not a taxi
utterly desolate
I have to walk about two kilometers
in the night and carrying
a heavy bag
to reach the center

seems like an invitation
to panic
which is fully ready
to lacerate me.

It's the seventh day of the heat wave
running between thirty nine
and forty-four
degrees Celsius.

I'm reached the midpoint
no trees in sight
no people either
I have to get out of here.

Yesterday's
announcements
on the evening news
quite horrific numbers
and details
coming in now
skin and bone
in my mind that is being consumed by fear.

All the houses
seem to be uninhabited
maybe they even have elderly corpses inside
who were left alone.

Every effort to speed up
makes it harder to breathe.

Miserable park with two or three benches
to my left
gives wings
to my morale
but I don't want
to stop
I have to
get out of this area.

11 November 1992

GAMES TIME PLAYS

A small whirlwind in the garden
as from the right hand
corner of the window
I hear the weather outside
that is those long forgotten sounds.

Running riot
the wind rages
such verbs
our mighty
Greek language
so lavishly provides
swept away
by each of its users and lovers.

Leaves of the bamboo
grove like flames
sky bronze
and the branches of the enormous pine
like arms of an outlandish figure
which from its height
is imploring
is threatening
or simply wanting
to make their
presence clear.

From the other corner
of the window
nothing.
You'd think it all
but figments of the
imagination.

22 September 1991

THE SPIRIT OF DEFENSE

> Pendant que les fonds publics s'écoulent en fêtes de fraternité, il sonne une cloche de feu rose dans les nuages.
> Arthur Rimbaud, *Illuminations*

That flying object
has never appeared again
and the terrible recollection of it
still turns me to stone
so I can hear that wind and see, that is,
vultures and airplanes
endure
the nonsense
and the combustion agreed on from above.

Oh bifurcated virtue
malicious nightmares.

1991

NOSTALGIA FOR THE FUTURE

A terrible energy
has declared that all gifts
shall be returned to earth.

Now I am constantly
traveling on ships and planes
and each place gives me
its humble help.

I would like to forget
those days
of prehistory
back when
the vegetable kingdom possessed
all the secrets
and omnipotent monsters
bordering on the ridiculous
sank into bogs.

I want to travel
on ships and planes
and with my mind rediscover
the small rose
at the frozen feet of the statue
the nostalgia for the future
set abloom.

5 July 1994

CHILDHOOD YEARS

> Le haut étang fume continuellement. Quelle sorcière va se dresser sur le couchant blanc? Quelles violettes frondaisons vont descendre?
> Arthur Rimbaud, *Illuminations*

IN THE PARK AT THE OLD PEOPLE'S HOME

Swept away
by the self-sufficiency of the clouds
a child of three and a half
in the park at the Old People's Home
scans the sky.

Now and then he bends to the ground
spends his time
observing
a line of ants
as they haul
a dead Gold Bug
whose shell
gleams greenly
they will lower it
to their kingdom
through a deep hole.

Frenzy seizes him
he digs in the ground
with his little shovel
that he can't handle
it keeps bending
till he puts it aside
and begins to dig with his hands
his ears, his nostrils fill with dirt
and time passes.

Now the two women
sitting there for so long
on the bench opposite
get up
they tell him it's time to go
the sun has set and they leave.

In time the face
of the older one has faded
the other, the young one,
is the mother and not forgotten.

The way back is far
removed from the old woman's bosom
a child of three and a half
looks at the hills of Tourkovounia
pulling away
Heaven is near
and Hell the same.

31 March 1995

HIGH FEVER

I was five years old
a high fever
on and off
from an unknown cause
three days in bed
in a coma.

Red ruled there
the reddest red I've ever known
complete detachment from
the realm of the familiar day
there were no pleasant games, sweets
but nor were there words that brought on nausea
an immersion and everything hot.

At some point it broke
and the day was normal again
autumn afternoon
when it darkens early and weighs on
children's hearts.
Father standing there at the corner
of the small bed
helped me climb back
to the world above
with a simple look.

19 December 1992

THE DECEMBER INCIDENTS*

St. Savvas and the Refugee Quarter
on Alexandras Avenue
walls pockmarked
by rockets fired from planes
holes as big
as fanlights.

New Year's afternoon
as we were eating
Pilchards canned baby squid
the whole place shuddered
the windows in the hall broke
a mortar had exploded in our garden
creation heavily charged with fear.

As soon as the shock passed
I went into the garden and found
pieces of the shell and its fins
the color of red lead
a bit like
the color of a baby squid
– but darker of course.

Every weapon has
its own bang.

1997

---

* The "December Incidents" refers to the outbreak of hostilities between the two sides in the Greek Civil War which began in December 1944 just one and a half months after the departure of the Germans, marking the beginning of a conflict that was to cause more Greek deaths than World War II itself and leave scars that last for decades.

LOUKIA

From the ashes of time
Loukia emerges
Loukia at the age of nine
in the house reading
raising Cain
with an upbringing I cannot grasp.

Unsmiling well-dressed
her ramrod straight father
scares me
and I know that the way I play
all day long in the streets
he thinks I'm riffraff
it doesn't bother me
but it hurts
not being able to see her.

When she sees me
her sad eyes
shine for a while
and then
a heavy shadow falls over them.

All afternoon I've been playing in this field
that's what it's called
but it isn't
a piece
of elevated earth
a forest of nettles
and a well they've sealed
with cornerstones.

And when I see her passing for a moment
behind the window
just like that I dive into the cold
to fend off

half a squeezed lemon
my friend positioned ten meters away
launches at me instead of a ball.

It's February
clear light
coming from Koulouri*
the bulging darkness
is coming on sowing
death.

Not that the lemon half
can be seen
in the darkness
it has by now become
a small dot
my hands hurt as I dive in
and instinctively
fend it off.

The day ended
Loukia's gone too
I'll go back to my home
bury myself in my books
because they have pictures
you can't get out of your mind
like the one of
Marko Kraljevic† with his companion
his horse a haunting image
in the night
as he patrols.
When I look at this picture

---

* Koulouri: a town on the island of Salamis. The island itself is also called by this name at times.
† Marko Kraljevic: a legendary Serbian hero. He died in 1395.

I immediately hear the boom
of the hooves of horses
I forget about Loukia for a while
and fall asleep
without fighting it.

24 February 1995

SOLITUDE SHARPENS THE SENSES

The day faints
in the light
while wild pigeons
exchange
messages in the air
which strike one as monotones.

1994

WHAT A PITY

No one comes to see and admire
this oasis
which a few

created for us
passing through
the pain of loss.

24 October 1995

THE ALTAR OF THE HOMELAND

> There the masses of
> fighting men pass,
> glorious sailors, of blessed memory
> valiant soldiers
> and serene mob.
>   A. Kalvos: *Lyrics*

Pilots of my country
never cease for one moment
intercepting
the airplanes of our neighbor
which violate
our air space.

16 October 1996

DELICATE BALANCES

Events may seem
irrevocable
acacias nevertheless
impart a luster
to the landscape which begins to disappear
as a sea of trash
swells unforgivingly.

28 April 1997

UNINHIBITED POEM

And I who had thought in the cafe
that the poem
did what I wanted it to
that I was the one subjected it to
the rhythms and glorious sounds
of Greek
suddenly realized
it was taking me
this way and that.

So, it turns out
I'm writing the way it wants:
poplars and clouds
armies, eleventh century,
the dry ravine,
hides tanning, Chios
and the enormous grief
when psychosis
engulfs your only daughter
while to the rear stand mothers taking care of things
well-intentioned as is the wind
which sanctifies
but as it moans and howls in the Cyclades
it maddens the cows
grazing in Neolithic meadows
and thus they too
add their own confusion
and strew panic around.

Hospital of the Most Blessed Virgin
and the cataract
not the one that delights the eye
in postcards
Niagara Falls, for example,
but the other one, the one
that dims the eye

and drives the mind inward
and in a flash
it's the sixteenth century
Orsini, Del Monte, the Borgias*
city-states, grey hills
midgets ascend toward heaven
to entertain themselves
with passions not confessed to…

The correlations in the sky
changed
the criteria gone mad
horrible weather
on Vasilissis Sofias Avenue
from what I can see
through the windows
of the cafe
a flock milling no guide at all
automobiles, umbrellas,
blurred image of the world.

1996

---

* Orsini, Del Monte, Borgia: names of the most powerful political and cultural families in 16th century Italy.

The Wild Boar Speaks
(2008)

AN IMPLACABLE IMAGE

Jeanne,
Maid of Orleans known as Joan of Arc
quite another thing
so innocent and as if stung
by her simplicity
the faces of the judges looming over her
the worst of all.

December 1995

STRANGE IDEAS

Strange ideas
jointly rule
my mind
with ambiguous images.

Understanding
a battle in the trees
rewarded by the beauty
of the unsullied landscape
the favor that was shown me
now and then seeing waves
on the filthy walls
and imaging a pink
there that doesn't exist
the final choice.

Suddenly day broke.
I can't remember what else.

23 July 1997

ELEGY FOR THE FALL OF
CONSTANTINOPLE

Spring was large and intense, heavy the light at night
and its gaunt face was bloodless.

One of ours made sinister by grand conceptions
reared amid the shade and the tumult
brought to head a thought of something that
for seven centuries now others would not have dared imagine.

His innermost motive was by no means a humble one
he wanted to kneel before the icon
all on his own in the dark on the left side of time.

And thus without water and the heart a sponge
he thought about method and counted the pauses
the masters slipped in and tapped him on the shoulder:

Come with us and live here since you like it so much
the icon of the Virgin Mary which we acquired
in a legal auction some seven hundred years ago.

And the sinister one brightened and his sword gleamed
he baffled their hearts and toppled the spineless ones

and they were saved whose Faith stood tall
the shipwrecked were rescued and dwarfs grew tall.

27 May 1972

THE CASTLE OF KYTHERA

Think of the castle
up in the Chora
of some island
Sifnos or Kythera
all the mystery
and all the plotting
when seen
there in the night
by pirates injured by the brine
and by the demon
of greed.

And think of those
who were inside
what agony
over their life
and their property
that would last as long
as it took
to prepare
for the pirates'
assault.

The cannonballs fell on the walls
holes opened everywhere
then those inside
lost their fear
and were possessed
by fury and rage.

As if I were seeing them
swept away
by the battle
first shooting
off arrows
then pouring scalding

oil
and all who got near
the embrasures
were sent toppling
as if they were
cloth dolls.

From the castle
that I see before me
but a few ruins
left and an old woman
selling herbs to foreigners
some see her
others don't
the sea is gleaming
like on the very first
of days.

12 October 2002

THE NIGHTMARES

So there he is
and no matter how free
the nightmares
hold him captive to his sleep.

Harridan standing
roughly four feet high
harridan who got in the
paternal house
harridan so ugly
she sows panic all
around her
chasing him
around the big table.

The commands crack
like horsewhips in the air
death is the first
jolt to reach the land
and then the man himself
trains which arrive wheezing
at stations with women and dust
and time running all the time
behind and ahead.

Tanks advance upon him
it seems that the Night
of the Epiphany has been revived, endless
all the monsters of Hades
have come out and chant.

Always the same landscape
looking west
first the hills
two of them, bare
and when you pass
untouched walls
what town is this
which century
from somewhere I know it
and then the sea
full of stones
a fouled sea
not to be seen
but as a feeling
many people in it swimming.

A wolfhound
at a gas station
has caught him
by his little toe
and won't let go
but there is a way
some mechanism
he'll pry open the jaws of the wolf
and his little toe
will be freed
people come running
make nervous motions
no solution is found
nor does it make any sense.

14 November 1975

IN MEMORY OF ONE WHO COMMITTED SUICIDE

> As I sit weighing and weighing
> my responsible Tristia.
> For what? For the ear? For the people?
> For what is said behind backs?
> \
> Seamus Heaney, *North*

Restless soul
like the willow on the plain
as the storm rages
and awe-bound man lies low.

Divine grace
did not endow him
with what we call a sense of measure
and when conditions converged
and buzzed round him like maenads
he found himself caught up in madness
in its own non-
figurative realm.

Everything got mixed up: Constantinople
solitude
the Mandzikert*
shadows on the wall
grandeur and derision.

---

* Mandzikert: town in Armenia, now part of Turkey. Where the Seljuk Turks defeated the Greeks for the first time in 1071 and the Byzantine Emperor Romanos Diogenes was taken prisoner.

Until that one day
he brought an end
to the confusion

with a bullet
and returned to the spirit world
where misgivings do not exist.

February 2000

REGGAE

The light commands
between wooden shacks
two men are fighting
dazed
they vent their rage
on the dirt road.

On the dirt road
two men are fighting
they vent their rage
dazed
the light commands
between wooden shacks.

Between the wooden shacks
two men fighting
on the dirt road
dazed
they vent their rage
the light commands.

8 October 1996

THE MILLENIUM NEARS ITS END

When the confusion all around
became the norm
sinful and inviolable
they came out of their lairs
ambiguous people
who beget
horrors and lies.

17 July 1997

THE POEM KNOWS NOTHING OF OBSTACLES

The children
had to be home
by sunset
a strict father
and customs were such
that in the village
no deviation was brooked.

Now thirty
years later
on television
a prostitute
begins her hard tale
the only way
she knows.

14 July 1997

RELATIVES OF THE VICTIMS ASCEND

In anguish and pain
they ascend
the snowy mountain road.
Cold and fatigue
have no power over them.

They are not mountain climbers
they are relatives
of those who were the passengers
on the airplane
and to whose wreckage they now
are headed
if they are allowed
to approach
by the rangers, firemen and soldiers
who have sealed off the site
of the accident.

19 May 1999

1998

Twelve months of sorrow
have collapsed in a heap, weighing me down
perhaps the low
sky is to blame
and the stubby cactus plants
on the balcony opposite
which remind me of monsters
those Gothic ones
on the Paris Notre Dame.

January 1999

QUESTION

When will we too enjoy your snow
and you our heat waves
without grumbling?

2002

COMMENTARY ON THE FIRST PART OF *THE DEER HUNTER*

Emigrant Orthodox Russians
set off from the very depths of their souls
to live in a landscape so reminiscent
of their paternal soil.

Steven Angela Mike
Linda Nikanor and others
their names escape me
but the grey weather
remains.
The branches are still bare
the town is called Clairton
smokestacks and noise.

Morning at the mill
earning of one's daily bread
and Saturday it's off to the woods
after first looking at the sun
to gauge by its rings
if the omens for hunting are good.

Now they climb the rocks
share in the knowledge
of unseen things
I climb along with them
to the cloud-shrouded summit.
And no grief of any kind casts a shadow on
the blessed screen
only the killing of the deer will disturb
the hearts of those there watching.

Two young people will get married
a reason for breaking the routine
of this small society
and yet he remains gloomy

the bride's father
who gets drunk every day
to drown who knows
what secret longing
on the night before the wedding
threatens to break it up
to slash everyone's tires
"They're all bitches, goddamn them"
he mutters to himself.

And when the time comes
the groom the holy sacraments the bride
relatives and friends
the priest saying, "I order Satan from here"
when the groom says
"Hold on, not yet",
the soul can no longer abide the body
looks for ways to escape,
and the rhythm of the film gallops off
taking us along…

February 2002

PARK IN STOCKHOLM

Someone is sleeping
under a plane tree
or a linden.

Someone lying on his back
is resting or
waiting for help
in this park in Stockholm.

Off to one side
small-bodied Asians play
electrified music
and women, marsh flowers,
roast meat.

Stockholm is ringed by water
inducing its inhabitants to reverie
but impenetrable granite
is everywhere present
under the light of the sun it favors cruelty
and at night hands out nightmares.

Likewise doubts are born
in love, in history,
and thus the man lying down
makes me wonder
if he is dreaming
or has surrendered
to the crushing weight of the granite.

10 January 2001

DAYS OF NOVEMBER 2003

> And a thick wind spreads round
> trash, dung, stench, and backbiting.
> George Seferis

A few days ago I was uneasy
about the weather that's come to make
whatever demands it had
pressured as well by necessity
and all the other thousand and one
glittering reasons
I was uneasy.

November arrived and on time
with two eclipses
and no rain
very dusty in the capital
chaos and confusion
and when night falls
on television I see
expediencies
squabbling
like vultures like old wives.

29 January 2004

OUTRAGEOUS POEM

Two cabbages behind the window
of the green-grocer's
like babies looking out at the world
the faint light is struggling
it is October and dust.

But at the evening meal
everything changed
reasonable conversations
flew back and forth
like bats.

It was like a celebration
before battle
the emotions
found no way out
the foreigners grew heavy with the wine.

Derailment
everything on red
at the extreme end of Europe
Belinda flew up
into the blue sky.

It seemed a most difficult undertaking
the atmosphere that night
in the little town of Novi Pazar
with the words that I am bringing to you.

27 March 2003

FLORENCE

Unbending architecture
which however the inhabitants
have warmed with their lives.

Santa Croce Square
with many shops and lean-tos
streets and tall houses
river of tourists
like a demonstration
ignorant of its course
in front a woman guiding
holding a cardboard
sign
Japanese outnumber all others
insatiable, tireless
disciplined
it's nearly noon
the cold bearable
Michelangelo doesn't interest me
he's too gigantic and doesn't fit in my heart
there are the others however which move us
and sharpen
emotions
we thought
had died
Bronzino for example
that is, his portraits
or Luca Signorelli
with his Christ Crucified and
Magdalene
the grief stays unchanged
down through the ages
nothing pompous
mystery and solemnity.

Yanna is tireless
thirsting to see
in the cafes we don't comment
on what we just saw
we will gaze at the clientele
such as the old man in a beret
a pre-war figure and somewhat in decline
the waiter speaks to him with respect
and he enjoys
the three women
who carry
large handbags from the fashion house.

December 2005

MEDELLIN

Columns and an orange
shed
everything set up
for the celebration
they check us
assiduously.

Yarouma* trees
so like a promise
that hasn't been kept
has been left hanging there
pending yet.

Red color
green walls
single storey houses
unsettled clouds
as soon as they disperse
Colombia
shines directly overhead.

December 2005

---

* Yarouma: tree with long white flowers growing high in the Andes in Colombia and elsewhere.

IN CONCLUSION

In the end fear is a bad smell
around me people
shut everything up or give in.

February 2000

THE WILD BOAR SPEAKS

So you see
I am everything you fear
but in some high-spirited ebullience
you want to fight it
in honest battle
with all the risk,
that Is, that you'll overpower it.

With the will of God
you made me a poem
let us turn then a new page
in our turbulent relations
and end this myth right here
that would immortalize death.

February 2000

Afterword

THE POETRY OF TASSOS DENEGRIS AND ITS "GENERATIONAL" AXES

TASSOS DENEGRIS (1934–2009) was born in Athens though his ancestral roots were in the island of Zakynthos. He studied cinematography at *Cinecittà* in Rome and was actively involved with the cinema both as a director and actor. He also held an official post at the Greek Press Office and later worked for a time in higher education, teaching literary translation in a special post-graduate program of the University of Athens. But above all else, through his seven collections of poetry, and the large number of vibrant translations to his credit Denegris was a *professional writer* with all that goes with that profession in Greece: a chronic lack of money and all the other sacrifices a writer must make, causing a number of predicaments for those who later studied his work. That is while he is admittedly one of the most distinguished Greek poets of the late 20th century, whenever one tries to place him within the existing literary-historical and literary schema of the period it proves to be, oddly enough, incredibly difficult.

I would say that this is largely the fault of the schema itself. Noted for its lack of a general theory, the historiography of Greek literature has uncritically adopted a system whereby its object is organized *by generation*. But it has never taken the trouble to make it clear the way it was using "generation": whether in its biological sense or in some other way, how long each one of these periods lasted and how the one succeeded the other. It does not even appear the critics have been aware that for some time in Europe there has been a well-developed *generational method* already in existence, founded historically by the German Julius Petersen and philosophically by the Spaniard José Ortega y Gasset. But as usual things here have continued to be ruled by improvisation and confusion: the "Generation of Demoticism" (1880) for example is defined based solely on a cultural cause (the "linguistic issue") as its cause, while that of the "Generation of Dissent" (1970) has revolved around the psychological and existential position taken by its members; the generations of the "20s", the "30s", the "80s" or the "90s", all allude to a changing of the guard (and the recruits) by decades while the so-called "First" and "Second" Post-War Generation set forth an academically suspect interpretation of intellectual and political history.

Is such a schema suited to Denegris? To a poet, that is, whom it is assumed we must assign to the "Second Post-War Generation" since his earliest poems date back to the beginning of the Fifties – though he was to put off his true debut for an entire decade – when he participated in the founding of the Greek avant garde through the *Pali* group – while his first book was only published in 1975 – during the "Generation of Dissent" and, in closing, during the final stage of his creative career he began to show some influences of the post-modernism prevalent at the end of the millennium. Obviously then this schema does not apply. That is, the relationship of Poetry with time has been shown to be far more complicated than any linear chronology can render, but in which academic philologists have incorporated it without the slightest qualm.

As the personal style is combined with various idiomatic elements in a textural linguistic "cocktail", the recipe for which only the poet himself knows, thus his "generational" basis is one that gathers together the hallmarks of multiple generations in a unique amalgam. The inner mechanism of similar compositions is directly connected to the manner in which each inheritance is managed. Harold Bloom, for example, referred to this matter by saying that poets are possessed by an "anxiety of influence" which more or less compels them into making anguished "miss-readings" through which they endeavour to try to wipe out every trace of debt to their forerunners. I personally believe that this influence is not only dealt with aggressively and competitively but also because of its "allure", the artist's aim being more or less to form a "partnership" and then incorporate it in a familiar creative undertaking. Whatever the case, the historical presence of the poet constitutes a challenge to History itself, since by subjugating the "generational" it tends to appear as a pristine event and unrepeatable.

Having said that, I am now ready to examine more analytically three "generational" starting points and three axes around which Denegris organized his poems.

1.

To begin with, in certain of his poems I have come upon an atmosphere, shall we say, let's call it *late symbolistic,* also containing a local reference to "Karyotacism" of the Twenties which was so unjustly disregarded by the poets of the next generation at the same moment these same poets were drawing their influences from him, and with complete correspondence, through the self-critical symbolism of Laforgue. Conversely Denegris valued (and exploited) duly the delicate Karyotakian mixture of "elegy and satire" as well as his ironic empathy for things which while they offer consolation for human pain also devalue it in a way by the fact these things are perennial:

> Leonardos at the age of ten
> racing along on his bike
> fell and scraped his knee
> he died in horrible pain
> the disease is called tetanus
> eight lines in the National Encyclopaedia.
> Little Leonardos must have been very lonely
> if one considers that his only friends
> were his dead grandfather
> whom he only knew about from tales
> and that red bicycle of his.
> Of the three only the bike remains
> locked away in a dark storeroom
> among photographs of wrestlers
> and rusty fishing gear.

(*The Example of Leonardos*, from Death in Kaningos Square, 1975)

Elsewhere the poet sets up a scenario of "protective enclosing", capable of exorcising the characteristic agoraphobia of the Symbolists ("Turn off the lights/Secure the door/Shut the windows"). Here the "Karyotakian" element appears in the dialectical function of the verb: its acoustic quality satisfies the quest of the Symbolists to approach music on the level of poetry plus the rather humoristic semantics involved in the rhyming of words which subverts their poetic nature itself.

In the preceding examples – and other similar ones – Denegris enters into a dialogue with the most profound part of the Karyotakian *modus operandi*, an unquestionable if distant imitation of his superficial technique. Things of this nature show the creative assimilation of the ancestral doctrine, and the complete subduing of the "anxiety of influence". Moreover, this also explains how a "generational" element which appears in the early work of Denegris was able to traverse his entire career. In order to convince ourselves that is indeed the case, let us return for example to "Epitaph for the Hated Murderer Douft" (from *The Spirit of Defence*, 1999) a ballad in which one finds distant echoes of the tone Karyotakis invented for his own "Michalio". One even present in his "Elegy" – there flavoured by the spirit of the demotic song – and well as in "Elegy on the Fall of Constantinople" (from the cycle *The Wild Boar Speaks*, 2009) where, following the same course, the poet transcends for all practical purposes any specific influence as he sets into motion narrative mechanisms without any narrative material.

I would go so far as to maintain that the ethos and the style of the "Karyotacism" in Denegris reminds one of the more daring experimenters in painting such as Picasso, for example, when he does a variation in his own way of *Meninas* by Velazquez.

2.

From time to time we have heard about the poet's supposed close relationship to the *beatniks*. This hypothesis is contributed to by the fact that in Greece, the age group to which Denegris belonged to did indeed take advantage of certain formal influences from the *Beat Generation*; furthermore the characteristic content of its poetry (for example what one finds in the imposing *Howl* by Allen Ginsberg) supposedly resembles the famous "dissent" which was the banner of the Seventies Generation (which coincided chronologically, and only in that way, with the first books by Denegris).

Nevertheless, it is not difficult to perceive that similar "undertakings" are little more than *petiones principii* without any other stimulus present and occasioned by the faulty use of the generational criterion one finds in Greek literary history. Furthermore, the sensitivity of Denegris is as different as could be imagined, by an unbiased reader, to that of the rage and violence of the American poets.

Despite all that, and while browsing through "my own" bibliography, that is the theoretical works which were of the most assistance to me and through which I acquired a clear and complete idea of recent and "modern" poetry, I discovered a certain typological relationship, or more precisely, a functional one, in the sense of the proportional function of two different historical and literary contexts.

More specifically, in the masterful *Los Hijos del Limo* ("The Children of Clay", 1974) by Octavio Paz, I find the idea expressed that the *Beat Generation* played a mainly *post festum* role – that is after World War II – in the avant garde that the Anglo-Saxon world had not experienced in the period between the wars. As it is now generally taken for granted, the Anglo-Saxon *High Modernism* – as it was developed by Eliot, Pound, Hulme and others – was a *classical revival,* whose aim was to bridge the chasm that had been opened by the Reformation between the English speaking part of civilization and the Greco-Roman inheritance of Roman Catholic Europe. It was against this recovered "classicism" of the great Modernist movement that the *Beat Generation* was reacting against, repeating (in a manner of speaking) the gestures the avant garde employed in the period between the wars. Because of that Paz goes on to suggest that the *beat* influence in countries which had experienced the historical avant garde appeared to be somewhat tautological.

The same can be said of Greece with the difference that the Greek avant garde of the period between the wars did not operate autonomously but was rather incorporated into the broader modernism of the Generation of the Thirties in which Seferis (as the mastermind behind that generation) gave it a classical touch, following the example of Eliot and Pound. The representatives of the literary historical phase, which reached its peak during the first half of the Seventies – Denegris being among those who took part – undertook the work of making the Greek avant garde autonomous and complete. I am referring here primarily to the group of young people which were centred around the magazine *Pali*.

I will not sketch in here the history of this specific group (which is more or less well known anyway) nor the activities of Tassos Denegris himself within this group. What I would like to stress here is that along with *Pali* – and because of his participation in *Pali* – Denegris belongs to (or belonged to when he started out) a mature avant garde movement suited to the needs of its Greek *context*, repeating – while at the same time clarifying – the profile of the one started in the period between the wars. This literary historical position and not the structural and stylistic characteristics of his writing, is the only thing which, in my opinion, could constitute the theoretical point of view by which someone could support a parallelism between our poet and the *Beat Generation*.

As for the rest, let me reiterate, the existential and aesthetic attitude of the *beatniks* (which if I am not wrong comes from the verb *to beat* – that is "to hit") differs radically from the corresponding characteristics of the poetry of Denegris. Except again if we advance on to the metaphoric interpretation of Andreas Embeirikos writing with the characteristic generosity he showed to the American poets, when (in the poem in the volume *Oktana* of the same name) he called them "*Beati* or The Non-Conforming Angels". In this sense Denegris is certain a *beato* (that is "blessed" in the theological terminology of Western Europe). It is also heavily influenced by that angelic spirit one feels in St. Francis of Assisi and the *beato* Jacopone da Todi.

Only that, for a present day poet, the profound love of the *beati* for Creation and its living things must pass through a world up in arms rather than just "non-conformity", a world that no longer contains such love. This is the real reason why I here quote a poem by the *beato* Tassos, which makes it clear that this angelic non-conformity is one he learned to denounce with a sarcastic candor, where the "word an orphan", exists in a world lacking in feeling, full of confusion and treachery:

> The word an orphan with no father
> gives way to delusion
> or the mailman driven
> to treacherous pursuits.
>
>
> The word an orphan with no mother
> it is sleek
> you may well admire it
> but it's heartless
> and shows no mercy
> and has never even had a whiff of
> love.
>
> ("Bluntly", *The State of Things,* 1989)

3.

As we have already seen, the first axis around which the poetry of Denegris began to be "generationally˙" structured was of a late Symbolist hue (Karyotacism), and the second brought in the element of the *post festum,* that is, the rejuvenation of the post war avant garde. The third "generational" factor, which brought to a close, so prematurely, the poet's creative cycle and his life as well, belongs to the sphere one could call *late modernity* (better known perhaps as "Post-Modernism"). The concept is not distinguished by a particular clarity and indeed suffers from a distinct semantic inflation, and for that reason needs to be clarified.

If in the present case, we can agree on something minimally acceptable, specifically that post-modernism is not a rude denial of modernism but rather its transcendence as well as that innovation in the aesthetic sphere means first and foremost the use of *irony,* then we must also accept the position of Octavio Paz, that in literature and art post-modernism projects the analogous inverse tendency toward *post-irony*. Put very simply, the former aims at change or the subversion of the established climate of evaluation and working in this direction characteristically resorts to the denial through affirmation and to affirmation through denial; the latter "is not interested in value as such, but the function of the "things themselves" and because of that they suspend the logic behind affirmation/denial and "bring opposites into communication with one another."

One has the impression that the inspired theoretical formulations of the Mexican poet describe the post-modern dimension in the poetry of Denegris, while the latter seems to occasionally produce variations, equally inspired, of these ideas fitted to his own poetic key. Proof of this is the following poem, "Essence of the Landscape":

> In this helplessness of the poet
> who has caught
> the beauty of the landscape
> in its entirety
> but isn't able
> or just doesn't want
> to convey it in words
> to our mind and your heart
> there is a certain grandeur.
> He triumphed over
> Illusion, which is
> what makes
> every poet want to
> fragment Essence
> so exaltation can benefit.
> glory to red
> honour to yellow
> giving everything they've got
> the moment the sun
> hides from our eyes.

(The State of Things, 1989)

Where there is no room for "exaltation" or even "delusion" from the moment the poet's words are expressed from within his silence and the colours of sunset have made their peace with the light that is going out.

Before concluding I would like to note my own conclusion that the "generational" axes which I have, perhaps, paid excessive attention to in my article do not correspond to "periods" in the poetry of Tassos Denegris, but to the *atmosphere* produced by his unique voice. Their final harmonization is a guarantee that this voice will continue to be heard for a long time yet and for just as long enchant us.

Victor Ivanovici

NOTE ON THE TRANSLATOR

Philip Ramp, a poet and translator, has been living in Greece for many years. He has translated a wide variety of Greek poets. Ramp's original poetry includes "JONZ" (Shoestring 1994), "BUTTE", "GLASS of an ORGANIC CLASS", "HOMING"(Pygmy Forest Press), "KEEN" (Shoestring 2007), and "QUITE"(Pygmy Forest Press 2010).

NOTE ON VICTOR IVANOVICI

Victor Ivanovici is Professor of Theory of Translation at the University of Thessaloniki, translator and literary critic.